GREECE

ISBN 960-213-019-9
Copyright© 1982
by
EKDOTIKE ATHENON S.A.
1, Vissarionos Street
Athens 106 72, Greece
PRINTED AND BOUND IN GREECE
by
EKDOTIKE HELLADOS S.A.
An affiliated company
8, Philadelphias Street, Athens

Publishers: George A. Christopoulos, John C. Bastias
Managing Editor: E. Karpodini-Dimitriadi
Translation: Alexandra Doumas
Layout: P. Pavlidou
Special Photography: N. Kontos, Y. Scouroyannis, M. Skiadaresis,
A. Spyropoulos, N. Stournaras, S. Tselentis

GREECE

A traveller's guide to the sites, monuments and history

E. Karpodini-Dimitriadi
Archaeologist

EKDOTIKE ATHENON S.A.
Athens 1999

Introduction

To make Greece's acquaintance is a great challenge. It is both easy and difficult. For nigh on two thousand years — since the days when the traveller Pausanias, in the second century AD *visited here — travellers and tourists have arrived in steady stream, all eagerly intent on getting to know something of its long history, its unique civilisation and enjoying its very special landscape. Very few countries offer such a variety of countryside and such a host of historical monuments; sunshine and light, high mountains, lushly verdant plains, coasts fringed with sandy beaches, brilliant white islands scattered with ancient ruins, interspersed with modern buildings, Greece is all these things. Home of the gods and heroes, persons fantastic and mythical, poets, orators, philosophers eternalise through space and time a historical continuum. Its name and its history are lost in the mists of legend. It was Homer who used the name "Hellas" for the first time, while in historical times the name "Hellenes" denoted not only the inhabitants of Central Greece, but also of Epirus, Macedonia, Thrace, Asia Minor, the isles of the Aegean and Ionian seas, as well as Southern Italy and Sicily.*

Since earliest times the land has been settled. The first traces of man at Petralona, Chalkidike are dated to the Middle Palaeolothic era (c. 50,000 BC*). During the Neolithic period, important cultural centres grew up, especially in Thessaly (Dimini-Sesklo), Crete, Attica, Central Greece and the Peloponnese. There was considerable socio-economic development, as well as artistic creativity, in the Bronze Age (circa 2000* BC*) and, indeed, during the final phase, the Late Helladic, generally known as the Mycenaean. Then it was that Mycenae "rich in gold" flourished, impressive palaces were constructed, Cyclopean fortifications built around their acropoles and works of art created, many of which have survived until the present day. Around 1100* BC *the Dorians descended upon Greece, irrevocably disrupting the indigenous population. Many fled to Asia Minor, while those who remained continued the development of the body politic, economic and cultural advancement. The Homeric poems give a picture of the society and institutions of that era (11th-8th century* BC*) during the latter part of which (9th-8th century* BC*) Geometric Art flourished. There was a smooth transition to the ensuing period — the Archaic, 8th-6th century* BC *— when there was an increased colonisation movement from Greece proper and the cities of Asia Minor to the shores of the Black Sea and to Sicily and Italy where Magna Graecia was established and where to this day Greek speaking enclaves still preserve the local dialects. In the same period a zenith was achieved in the arts - sculpture and architecture - and especially in pottery and vase-painting. Then it was, too, that the city state acquired its definitive form. The 5th and 4th century* BC *constitute the Golden Age, the Classical Miracle. Then the* *influence of Athens radiated everywhere, for here flourished letters, arts, theatre and philosophy and political institutions were formed, culminating in the triumph of Democracy. Then it was that the united Greek cities won a brilliant victory over the Persian invaders (490-479 BC). The increasing political power of Athens and its rivalry with Corinth and Sparta was one of the several causes of the catastrophic Peloponnesian War (431-404 BC) which struck a mortal blow to the development of the cities and civil strife sapped them of their strength. Cultural development was not curtailed; indeed with the domination of the Macedonians, first with Philip II (359-336 BC) and then with Alexander (336-323 BC), it was reinforced. On Alexander's death the vast empire he had created passed to his successors, who divided it into states. In Greece proper there was an alliance of confederations (Aetolian-Achaian) which did not manage to unite the cities and so brought about the intervention of the new power of Rome, by which they were subjugated, (146 BC). However, the spirit and soul of Greece made such an impression on its conquerors that they strove to emulate the achievements of the Classical era in the arts and were careful to embellish their conquered regions with monuments, many of which are still extant. From AD 395 Greece constituted part of the Byzantine empire and many cities reached their apogee (Patras, Corinth), became intellectual and centres (Mystras) or commercial (Monemvasia, Nauplion) ones. During this period barbaric and piratical incursions were a constant plague throughout the land. With the Fourth Crusade and the Sack of Constantinople by the Franks (1204), Greece was divided into Frankish and Venetian states, while a very few areas still remained in Byzantine hands (Despotate of Epirus). In order to consolidate their power, the conquerors built or repaired imposing fortresses. Some of the most impressive are in the Peloponnese (Mystras, Monemvasia, Methone, Korone, Chlemoutsi), as well as those of the islands. The Fall of Constantinople to the Turks (1453) brought new adventures and misfortunes which the Greeks endured until the War of Independence, with which they won their freedom (1821). The first capital of the independent state was Nauplion; only later was it transferred to Athens. However, the Greeks never ceased to struggle for the progress and advancement of their state.*

Along with the light, sun, sea, friendly inhabitants, quaint customs and festivals, the modern visitor will also get to know Greece's mythical and historical past, which the labours of archaeologists have brought to life. For, as the French Academician Michel Déon has written, in Greece contemporary man, so often disorientated, discovers a quite incredible joy; he discovers his roots.

Attica — *Athens*

Capital of Greece, one of the oldest in the world (first inhabited circa 6000 BC). The visitor to the fortified Acropolis is confronted with a variety of impressions. One can admire the "monument of monuments", the **Parthenon, temple of Athena,** which was built in the era of Pericles (447-432 BC) by the architect Iktinos and embellished by Pheidias. There are other wonderful edifices on the Acropolis: the **temple of Athena Nike** (420 BC), the **Erechtheion** with its unique karyatids which supported the porch of the temple (nowadays in the museum), the **Propylaia,** which to this day constitutes the entrance to the Acropolis, the sacred rock. Exhibited in the **Acropolis Museum** are unique sculpted compositions, dating from Archaic (8th-6th century BC) to Roman times.

Among the sights of Athens are the **Theatre of Dionysos** (on the south slope of the Acropolis) where productions of drama were staged in antiquity, and the **Odeion of Herodes Atticus,** where even today, throughout the summer festival season, musical and theatrical performances are given. On the northwest side of the Acropolis one may wander amidst the ruins of the **Ancient Agora** (market place) of Athens, which in antiquity was the focus of the most important activities of Athenian life (religious, political and philosophical) and where there existed sanctuaries, stoas and diverse cult buildings, as well as "ex votos". Here stands the **temple of Hephaistos** (Theseion), the best-preserved ancient temple, built between 449 and 444 BC, which was used in Christian times as a church of St. George. By far the most impressive building is the restored **Stoa of Attalos,** which nowadays houses the Agora Museum, with finds mainly coming from the Agora excavations. To the northeast are the remains of the **Roman Forum,** including the **Tower of the Winds,** Kyrrhistos' clock. Nearby are the ruins of **Hadrian's Library** (AD 132). West of the Acropolis are the low hills of the **Pnyx** and the **Areios Pagos,** as well as the Hill of the Muses with **Philopappos' monument** (2nd century AD).

One of the loveliest and best-preserved choregic monuments is that of Lysistrates (335-4 BC), to the east of the Acropolis and a short distance from it is **Hadrian's Arch,** which separated the Classical city from the Roman. Nearby are the impressive columns of the temple of **Olympian Zeus** (begun in 515 BC and completed in AD 131). To the environs of Classical Athens belongs **Kerameikos,** the municipal cemetery of ancient Athens in which one can nowadays see Classical funerary monuments and grave stelae still standing on either side of the road leading from the Sacred Gate, while finds from the excavations there are displayed in the museum. Other monuments of the Classical period include the **temple of Poseidon** on the promontory of **Sounion** from where one can enjoy a romantic sunset, as well as the sanctuary of Artemis at **Brauron** (there is a museum with local finds) and the sanctuary of Demetra at **Eleusis,** renowned in antiquity as the cult site of the Eleusinian mysteries. Finds from the excavation are on show in the museum. **Marathon, Ramnous** and **Oropos** with its sanctuary of Amphiaraos are other places of historical interest having Classical monuments. There are unique treasures from Prehistoric to Roman times in the **National Archaeological Museum** of Athens. Outstanding are the Mycenaean gold face masks, the wall paintings of Thera, the giant kouros of Sounion, Poseidon of Artemision, the Youth from Antikythera et al. There are several other museums in Athens: the **Byzantine, Historical and Ethnological**, and **Benaki** Museum, the **Museum of Folk Art**, Numismatic and the **National Art Gallery.**

Monuments of the Byzantine era are preserved within the actual city: (Panaghia Gorgoepikoos, Kapnikarea, Aghioi Theodoroi, Aghioi Asomatoi, Sotira Lykodemos), as well as on the outskirts (Kaisariani), while the most significant is **Daphni,** the mosaics of which are the finest examples of Byzantine decoration. Its architecture constitutes the most representative example of an octagonal church of the 11th century.

Modern Athens is a big city, the centre of which is **Constitution Square,** surrounded by contemporary buildings, luxury hotels and, opposite, the **Greek House of Parliament** and the monument of the Unknown Soldier with its honorary guard of Euzones. From the summit of **Lycabettos Hill** one has a panoramic view of the entire area. A few impressive Neoclassical buildings still survive in Athens: the **National Library**, the **University** and the **Academy**, all three designed by Th. Hansen, the **Polytechneion,** the building of the **National Museum** and **Zappeion.** Mention should also be made of the **Stadium,** located on the site of the ancient stadium, which was totally restored in 1896 for the first Olympic Games. The quarter known as **Plaka** maintains its picturesqueness and peculiar "couleur local", with its narrow streets and amusement centres, as well as **Monastiraki** with its numerous tourist shops.

From antiquity to the present day, **Piraeus** has been the port of Athens and is now the largest harbour in the country. Ancient remains are very few, while the finds from excavations are housed in the Archaeological Museum. There is also a Maritime Museum. Along the length of the shore one can see traces of the ancient fortifications, while nearby at the port of Zea are ruins of the ancient theatre. Without doubt the most picturesque parts of Piraeus are its yacht harbours, and the hill of Kastella.

The islands of the Saronic Gulf

From Athens one can easily get to know the islands of the Saronic Gulf: *Figs. 18-22* **Aegina** with its temple of Aphaia, **Salamis** (the nearest) in the Straits of which the Greeks defeated the Persians (479 BC), **Hydra** with its strange landscape and architecture of its houses, and the charming little island of **Spetses.**

Peloponnese

Figs. 23-56   There are many ways of reaching Greece's largest peninsula, with its beautiful countryside, its resorts (summer and winter), its idyllic coast. The most usual route is via the Isthmus, from antiquity till nowadays the border between Attica and the Peloponnese. The canal, which was opened (1881-1893) followed an ancient precedent, since the tyrants of Corinth (7th century BC) had actually envisaged such an undertaking. The history of the region is lost in the depths of prehistory: here developed the most important cities of the ancient world and the most important sanctuaries. What should one see first? Just before the Isthmus is **Loutraki** with its harbour Vouliagmeni and the picturesque site of the **Heraion at Perachora, Isthmia,** just beyond the Isthmus, where Panhellenic games were held every two years, **Corinth,** the wealthy and mighty city which was destroyed by the Romans (146 BC) only to be rebuilt by the same (Julius Caesar 44 BC), where are preserved temples and buildings in the area of the agora, where the archaeological museum with its local finds is housed. Looming over the city is the imposing hill of **Acrocorinth** with its medieval fortress. Proceeding southwards, on a bare hill stand the ruins of **Mycenae,** the powerful acropolis of king Agamemnon which flourished in the 14th century BC and whose influence reached as far as Crete, the shores of Egypt and the West, creating the unique "Mycenaean civilisation". Close by (6 kms.) stands yet another historic town with monuments and a museum, **Argos,** and to the south is the Cyclopean acropolis of **Tiryns,** 5 kms. before **Nauplion,** the lovely town which retains its old-world atmosphere with its fortresses, houses and narrow streets. One of the most frequented sites is **Epidaurus** (30 kms. beyond Nauplion) with its famous well-preserved theatre (4th century BC) and the remains of the sanctuary of Asklepios.

   Sparta, the home of Leonidas, is today a modern town dominated by the impressive mass of Mount Taygetos. **Mystras,** the deserted citadel (5 kms. outside Sparta) preserves an atmosphere all its own, as does the peculiar rock of **Monemvasia** (40 kms. SE) with its small town enclosed by ramparts. Among the outstanding regions is **Mani** with the amazing caves in Dyros and the castles of **Korone** (50 kms. beyond Kalamata) and **Methone** (about 20 kms. beyond Pylos). The famous palace of King Nestor was discovered 15 kms. NE of Pylos while **Olympia,** one of the most ancient centres of the Peloponnese where Panhellenic games were held every four years, overwhelms one with its host of buildings in the ancient sanctuary and the wealth of finds in its museum. One of the most memorable exhibits is the statue of Hermes with the infant Dionysos, work of Praxiteles, the sculptures from the decoration of the temple of Zeus, the clay group of Zeus with Ganymede and the collection of bronze objects. On the plateau of **Bassae** is preserved one of the most beautiful ancient temples dedicated to Apollo. **Patras,** crossroads and third harbour of

Greece, is an ideal starting point for the islands of Zakynthos, Kephalonia and also Central Greece. To the south of the Peloponnese is the very lovely island of **Kythera.**

Central Greece

Central Greece (Sterea Hellas) not only offers a change of landscape but also of monuments (Naupaktos, Mesolongi, Leivadia, Thermopylae, Itea, Galaxidi). The most important site to visit is **Delphi,** with its impressive remains from the ancient sanctuary of Apollo, to which came gifts and votives from those seeking an oracular prophecy. Some of the decorative members of the monuments, as well as the votives, can be seen in the museum. The charioteer is the most superb of all. *Figs. 57-69*

Hosios Loukas, just before Delphi, provides an example (one of the very few still remaining) of Byzantine architecture of the 11th century and, with its numerous mosaics, of ecclesiastical decoration.

Thessaly

The historic plain with its ancient settlements (especially interesting are Neolithic Sesklo and Dimini, outside Volos), the fertile vale of Tempe and the imposing mountain range of Olympos, the mythical home of the gods, has two regions of unique beauty: **Meteora** (outside Trikala) and **Pelion.** The weird rock formations of Meteora, on which nestle monasteries and hermitages, constitute a unique spectacle, while the monasteries contain valuable treasures. Pelion, with its picturesque villages and high, verdant environment is serene and pleasant all months of the year, a state difficult to find elsewhere. *Figs. 73-85*

Epirus

Here the landscape is exclusively mountainous and there are both ancient sites (**Dodona,** with its ancient theatre, **Kassope, Nikopolis**) and historical cities (**Ioannina, Parga, Arta**), as well as areas which immortalise the rich folk tradition (**Metsovo**). Of especial interest is the stalagmite and stalactite decoration of the Perama caves at Ioannina. Epirus has wonderful resorts, winter and summer, as well as regions of incomparable natural beauty. *Figs. 120-129*

Macedonia

The most extensive region of Greece, it is distinguished by its fertile *Figs. 86-119* plains, rich rivers and numerous historic sites, where new finds are always coming to light (Petralona, Olynthos, Pella, Sindos, Dion, Vergina). Its capital, **Thessalonike,** known as the bride of the north, is nowadays divided into the old town (ano Polis) and the contemporary one with its modern buildings. Here one can visit Roman monuments, many Byzantine ones and churches (Aghios Dimitrios, Rotonda, Panaghia Chalkeon), the White Tower, the archaeological museum and take excursions into the suburbs. The peninsula of **Chalkidike** with its endless beaches, rich green hinterland and little villages offers a unique experience. Here is located the monastic state of **Mount Athos** with its wild landscape and inestimable treasures in its many monasteries, as well as the cave of Kokkines Petres (Petralona) in which were found organic remains and the famous human cranium of Neanderthal man.

Sites of historical and archaeological interest include **Pella,** with the well-preserved mosaics in its houses, **Sindos, Dion** and, first and foremost, **Vergina** where the recent investigations of Professor M. Andronikos have brought to light unique treasures from the unplundered tombs of the capital of the kings of Macedon. Places of great natural beauty are **Edessa,** with its waterfalls, **Veroia, Naousa,** idyllic **Kastoria** and **Florina** with the nearby lakes of Prespes. **Kavala** is also an interesting town with the nearby ancient city of **Philippi.** One can pass from Keramoti to the opposite densely-wooded island of **Thasos,** with its rich vegetation and quiet beaches, a veritable paradise.

Thrace

Inhabited since prehistoric times, Thrace played a decisive role in all periods of Greek history. In its towns are preserved many traditional houses, in and amongst the inevitable modern buildings. Close to **Xanthi** is **Avdira** home of Demokritos, of the sophist Protagoras and also of poets, historians and philosophers. **Komotini** (with an archaeological museum) is built beside the ancient Egnatian Way. From **Alexandroupolis,** capital of the province, one can sail across to **Samothrace,** with its fine countryside. One of the finds from excavations on the island is the famous statue of the Victory (Nike), in the Louvre Museum.

Ionian islands

Figs. 130-140   The islands are among the loveliest spots in Greece, instilling a sense of wonder and excitement in all who visit them.

Strung out one after the other, close to the shores of Western Greece, the Ionian islands offer a diversity of environment and monuments. The largest is **Corfu** (Kerkyra), the Homeric isle of the Phaeceans, which has monuments from the 15th to 18th century, buildings of Venetian inspiration and others from the days of English sovereignty and French rule. Its quaint alleys form an unusual picture, as do the regions outside the town with panoramic views, sandy shores and dark green hillslopes. The local festivals are most spectacular. Finally, the **Achilleion** palace, nowadays the casino, attracts numerous visitors, as does the **archaeological museum,** the **Sino-japanese** collection and the **Art Gallery.** Other Ionian islands are equally picturesque: **Paxoi, Antipaxoi, Leukada, Ithaca,** the home of Homeric Odysseus, **Kephalonia,** the largest in area with attractive countryside as well as historical monuments, and **Zakynthos,** with its delightful landscape, many sandy beaches and host of monuments.

Aegean islands

All along the length of the coast of the mainland of Greece extends **Euboea,** with its dense green woods and olive trees. From the north side of the island one can cross to **Skyros,** one of the fascinating islands of the Sporades with its cuboid houses on the hill slope dominated by the castle. **Alonissos** also belongs to the Sporades, as does picturesque **Skopelos** and lushly verdant **Skiathos.** The Sporades belong to the islands of the Aegean sea, cradle of the most ancient civilisation. Small islands are dotted about, with brilliant white houses, picturesque shores, and small delightful villages which cover the historical continuity from prehistoric times to the present day.

*Figs. 70-72,
153-164*

Islands of the Northeast Aegean

These include **Limnos,** with its historic towns and lovely beaches, **Lesbos,** one of the largest Greek islands with coastal villages, green forests, fantastic landscapes. Home of the ancient lyric poets, it immortalises its cultural and artistic tradition. Another of these islands is **Chios** whose long history is lost in myth. In the capital town one can see the ancient city with its walls and theatre and visit the museums. In the countryside the monastery "Nea Moni" with its unique Byzantine mosaics is worthy of attention as is Pyrgi with its scheduled medieval houses. **Samos** home of the philosopher Pythagoras, with its famous temple of Hera (Heraion) and **Ikaria,** with its therapeutic thermal springs, together with **Oinouses** and **Psara** complete the island complex.

Figs. 141-152

Cyclades

It is difficult for one to describe the beauty of the Cyclades, with their very long past, renowned civilisation (Cycladic), the legends which are in-

Figs. 165-210

termingled with the present and brought to life at every step, the picturesque brilliant white houses, slender windmills, windswept cliffs, stones glistening in the sun, the endless sandy beaches and monumental remains of all periods. The principal ones are: **Mykonos,** nowadays an international tourist centre, **Delos,** home of Apollo and Artemis, religious and cultural centre in antiquity, today an enormous archaeological site, **Tinos,** isle of the Virgin (Panaghia), ever-green **Andros,** the capital **Syros,** with its Neoclassical houses and amphitheatral architecture, **Paros,** one of the largest and home of the Panaghia Katapoliani, with serene landscape and endless beaches, **Antiparos** with its impressive cave, **Naxos,** the largest island in area with quiet and beautiful countryside, **Amorgos** with its distinctive Cycladic architecture, **Anaphi, Ios** with its many chapels and unique quaintness, **Santorini** (Thera) where excavations have brought to light astonishing finds and an entire prehistoric city with its streets and houses, the latter decorated with wonderful wall paintings. The west Cyclades include **Melos,** isle of Aphrodite, **Kea, Kythnos, Kimolos, Seriphos** and **Siphnos** with its little villages where lovely pottery is manufactured and its sparkling white houses, fine examples of unspoilt Cycladic architecture.

Dodecanese

Figs. 211-230 They were thus named because the major islands are twelve in number. The best-known is **Rhodes,** which with its virtually uninterrupted sunshine, its antiquities and its incomparable landscape is one of the most islands with tourists. The town of Rhodes preserves a distinctly medieval colour in its houses, streets and even more so in its popular buildings from the time of the knights. Examples of the cultural and artistic tradition of the island are exhibited in the museums (archaeological, folk art and art gallery) while ancient ruins have survived on the acropolis of ancient Rhodes. There are enchanting spots all over the island (Rhodini, Kallithea, Valley of the Butterflies), as well as many of historical interest (Kamiros, Philerimos), outstanding amongst them being Lindos where the picturesque village is dominated by the awe-inspiring ancient acropolis with its fortifications which were repaired and extended by the Knights and the Turks. **Kos** is known as the home of Hippokrates, father of medicine. Monuments from its rich historic past are preserved everywhere. Particularly picturesque is **Symi,** as is **Kalymnos,** while **Patmos,** the island of the Apocalypse (here lived John the Apostle and wrote his Revelations in the homonymous cave) offers a unique picture of beauty as it is dominated by the fortified monastery. A rich historic past, monuments, as well as solitude and charming bays characterise **Leros, Nisyros, Tilos, Astypalaia** and far-flung **Kastellorizo, Kasos** and **Karpathos** with its extraordinary countryside, dreamlike beaches, which make a lasting impression on all who visit them.

Crete

Greece's largest island with not only a long history, cultural tradition *Figs. 231-265* and host of monuments, but with an incomparable environment which varies from extremely mountainous to flat plains. Considerable contemporary development enables one to spend carefree and relaxing vacations, though Crete is not without regions where traditional conditions ensure the intact survival of the Cretan soul.

Home of the mythical king Minos, a splendid civilisation grew up there, the Minoan, examples of which are preserved in the archaeological sites and Herakleion museum. Traces of all phases of its history have survived throughout the island, especially of the Middle Ages. In **Herakleion,** medieval Candia, there are many interesting sights. Exhibited in its museum are finds which provide a panorama of Cretan civilisation. The archaeological site of **Knossos** (5 km. outside Herakleion) with its daedalic ruins of the Minoan palace, restored parts and royal throne, is without doubt most impressive. Remains of Minoan palaces, as well as of Minoan villas, are preserved at **Phaistos, Malia, Zakros, Tylissos, Aghia Triada,** while the unplundered cemetery at **Archanes** has produced numerous finds. One can get to know the face of contemporary Crete at **Lasithi,** with its many windmills. **Elounda** and **Aghios Nikolaos** with its tiny harbour attract their own admirers, as do **Siteia, Myrtos** and the charming little town of **Rethymnon** with its rich past and the nearby historic monastery of **Arkadi. Chania** with its Byzantine castle, houses and narrow streets preserves the most markedly medieval character. **Samaria** with its unique and astonishingly beautiful gorge gives one inexpressible satisfaction. Crete's interest is inexhaustible for at every step one may discover other aspects of its beauty, coupled with its history and rich folk tradition.

*1. The Parthenon, monument of monuments as it has been called, dominates the
Acropolis. It was built between 447-432 BC and dedicated to the goddess Athena, patron
deity of the city. Three great names are connected with it: Pericles, who inspired it, as he
did the entire building programme on the Acropolis, Pheidias, general supervisor of the
works and Iktinos, its architect. The Pentelic marble temple combines Ionic features with
the principal Doric ones and has an aura of magnificence and grace. Peripteros (8
columns on the narrow sides and 15 on the long ones) with pronaos, cella and adyton it
presented, thanks to its rich sculpted decoration (pediments, metopes), an incomparable
aesthetic experience. Within the cella stood the gold and ivory statue of Athena, work of
Pheidias. Despite its destruction and plunder during the course of the centuries the
temple still retains its imposing splendour.*

Acropolis — *Temple of Athena Nike, Erechtheion*

2. The small amphiprostyle temple of Athena Nike (there are only 4 columns on each narrow side) was built on the northwest side of the rock of the Acropolis during the Peloponnesian War (427 - 424 BC) on the spot where the goddess was worshipped of old. From its rich decoration only some of the figures of the frieze, the subject of which was the conflict between the Greeks and Persians, have survived.

3. The Erechtheion. This architecturally idiosyncratic temple was built on the most sacred spot on the rock where, according to mythological tradition, Athena and Poseidon participated in a contest to determine who was to be protector of the city which spread out around the rock. The most impressive part of the temple was its porch with the Karyatids, slenderbodied maidens who supported its porch (nowadays in the museum) which emanated beauty and grace.

Acropolis

4. The Acropolis and
partial view of the city of
Athens. On the surface of
the impressive hill,
fortified since earliest
prehistoric times, were
accumulated artistic
masterpieces which still
move their beholders.
Today only foundations of
the diverse buildings, some
of them unique
monuments, are preserved;
the Parthenon, the
Erechtheion, the temple of
Athena Nike, the
Propylaia and
Pinakotheke, creations of
the Golden Age of ancient
Athens. Preserved on the
southwest slope is the
theatre built by Herodes
Atticus (2nd century AD)
where, even today, musical
and theatrical
performances are held.
The Stoa of Eumenes
(2nd century AD), which
connects the Odeum of
Herodes Atticus with the
ancient theatre of
Dionysos, where ancient
dramas are performed,
has also survived.

Ancient Agora

5. *Partial view of the ancient agora with the restored Stoa of Attalos in which the museum is housed. The Agora was the centre of ancient Athenian life, social and political. Here Socrates and Plato taught philosophy, and here democracy was born. The area of the agora was embellished with many buildings and votives, of which the foundations and bases have been revealed and traces have survived.*

5

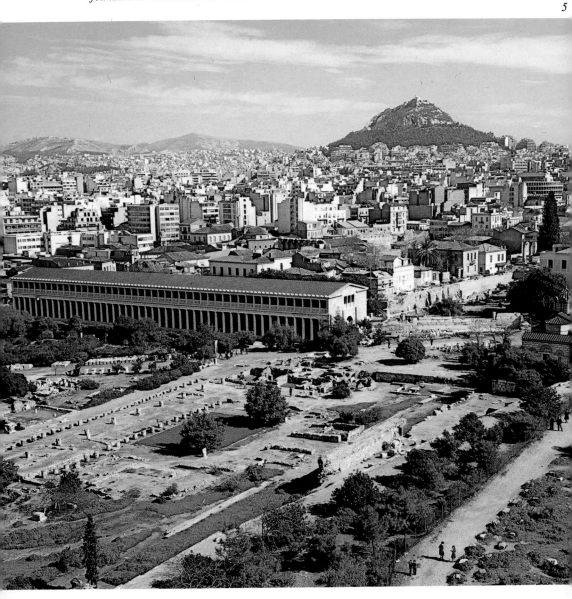

Philopappos' Hill, Acropolis

6. *Low hills rise west of the Acropolis from where one has a wonderful view of the sacred rock, as well as of the city of Athens. One of them is the hill of Philopappos, or the hill of the Muses, dominated by the homonymous funerary monument, built by Philopappos from Syria, who became an Athenian and benefactor of the city, in the 2nd century* AD. *This marble monument, is decorated with relief representations.*

6

7

Temple of Olympian Zeus

7. *The Olympieion and partial view of Athens with the Acropolis in the background
(right) and Philopappos' Hill (left). Construction of this impressively large temple, which
was dedicated to Olympian Zeus, commenced in 515 BC, though it was not completed
until AD 131-132 in the reign of the Roman emperor Hadrian. During the intervening
period it changed from the Doric order to the Corinthian. Of the original 104 columns
only 15 are still extant, as well as the drums of a few more which have fallen to the
ground. Within the sanctuary several ancient buildings have been unearthed, while the
western edge is dominated by Hadrian's Arch, built in honour of the emperor Hadrian,
which divided the ancient city from its Roman extension.*

8. *Lycabettos Hill from where one has a panoramic vista of the plain of Athens.*

9. *The Byzantine monastery of Kaisariani is situated a few kilometres from the centre of Athens. Built in the 11th century and dedicated to the Presentation of the Virgin, nothing has survived of its original wall paintings. The existing murals belong to later periods. The monastery and ancillary buildings of the complex are located in a uniquely beautiful environment which offers solitude and serenity.*

10. *Daphni, the most important Byzantine monument in Athens with its astonishing mosaics. The monastery was built on the very spot where Apollo was worshipped in the 5th century BC and was enlarged in stages. The monastery fortification, buildings and large octagonal church can be seen today.*

8

Piraeus

*11. Piraeus, the harbour
of Athens since antiquity.
In addition to the central
harbour of Piraeus, one
can see here Mikrolimano,
the harbour of Zea and
the Akti peninsula, on
which sections of the
ancient defensive walls
which surrounded Piraeus
are preserved. In the
background is the island
of Salamis.*

Sounion, Eleusis

12. Cape Sounion with the temple of Poseidon. The temple was built between 444 and 440 BC on the site where a cult of the god had existed since early times. It is Doric, peripteral (13 columns on the long sides and 6 on the narrow ones) and bore sculpted decoration with mythological subjects. Today only 15 of the original columns and a very small part of its sculptured decoration have survived. To the northeast stood the temple of Athena, the foundations of which are preserved. The temple of Poseidon has impressed and continues to impress all who visit it, or behold it from the sea. One of its most illustrious visitors was Lord Byron, who even inscribed his name on one of the door jambs. Sightseers are numerous today; many of them come to enjoy the romantic sunset seen from here.

13. The archaeological site of Eleusis where the goddess Demetra was worshipped in special occult festivals and secret rites. Non-initiates were banned from participating in these rites and initiates were not permitted to divulge the "sacred sayings" or symbolic acts of the mysteries. Nowadays a few remains of the buildings have survived but the foundations are in a dreadful state of preservation due to the industrial pollution of the area.

13

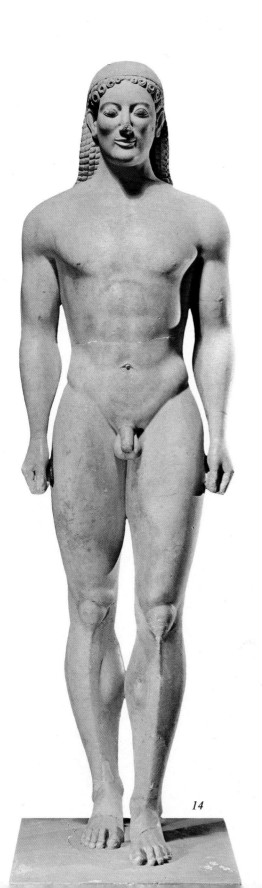

Archaic and Classical Sculpture

From the 7th century the Greeks, influenced by eastern prototypes, set up within their temples statues of stone and marble. As time passed these statues were transformed, aquired life and movement and began to be erected in sanctuaries and on graves. Statues of Kouroi and Kores, some of them painted, funerary reliefs, sphinxes and heads testify to an art which developed into the Classical miracle. Beginning with the rendering of the type of nude youth, Kouros, the artists achieved the sculpted perfection of Classical times. Alongside the marble statues, the bronze ones are also outstanding, being infused with an expressiveness and "inner mystic style", despite the coldness of the metal.

14. Kroisos, Kouros of 530 BC from Anavyssos, Attica (Athens, National Archaeological Museum).

15. The youth of Antikythera, detail. A bronze statue of a young man found in the sea off Antikythera and dated to circa 340 BC. The statue emanates unique strength and grace.

16. The Kore with almond eyes, detail. This is one of the loveliest female statues (Kores), votive to Athena about 500 BC, one of the most characteristic exhibits in the Acropolis Museum.

17. Marble relief plaque from the east side of the Parthenon frieze. Poseidon, Apollo and Artemis are represented in all their divine power and magnificence.

14

15

16

17

The islands of the Saronic Gulf

Aegina — Temple of Athena Aphaia

18. The temple of Aphaia on Aegina. It is Doric, peripteral (6 columns on the narrow sides and 12 on the long) and was built on a cult site in use from prehistoric times. It acquired its final form around 500 BC, when the entire sanctuary area was laid out. The greater part of the temple was built of local limestone, while some of its members were also painted, as were the sculptures of the Parian marble pediments and acroteria. The compositions of the pediments had as their subject battles of the Trojan War at which Athena was present and are distinguished by their precision of execution and expressiveness. The temple of Athena comprised a harmonious entity.

19. View of the picturesque island of Aegina. The island, which has been inhabited since Neolithic times, was named after Aegina, daughter of the river Asopos, who was brought there by Zeus. It has a rich mythological and historical tradition and on it can be seen monuments of all eras, the temple of Aphaia Athena being outstanding among them. It also offers a verdant landscape and countless coves with beautiful sandy beaches.

Hydra — Spetses — Poros

20. Hydra, known in antiquity as Hydraia, has been continuously settled since Prehistoric times. With their great maritime tradition its inhabitants made a tremendous contribution to the War of Independence. The town of Hydra constitutes a pleasant surprise when one first catches a glimpse of it with its high houses climbing up the arid, barren rock, narrow steep streets and picturesque harbour.

21. Spetses, yet another island in the Saronic Gulf, lushly verdant with lovely houses, pebbled courtyards and two harbours, Dapia and the old harbour, presenting a unique aesthetic experience.

22. Poros is the closest island of the Saronic Gulf to the mainland. In antiquity it was known as Kalavreia and Poseidon was worshipped here. Thanks to its lush vegetation, mild climate and beautiful environment it is very popular with visitors.

20

23. The Isthmus of Corinth, the Link between the Peloponnese and Sterea Hellas. The first attempts to cut a canal were made in antiquity, but were not realised until quite recently (1881-1893).

23

2

24. View of the agora of ancient Corinth with the paved Lechaion road, ruins of shops and the hill of Acrocorinth in the background. Corinth was one of the most important cities of ancient Greece and was razed to the ground by the Romans (146 BC) only to be rebuilt by them in 44 BC. It is to this period that the majority of remains are dated.

25. The ancient temple of Corinth (6th century BC) which was dedicated to Apollo. Nowadays only 7 of its 21 monolithic Doric columns, those on the north and west side of the peristyle, survive.

26. *Aerial photograph of the fortified acropolis of Mycenae, capital of king Agammemnon. The Cyclopean rampart, Grave Circle A and the palace at the summit are visible. Mycenae was the cradle of one of the most splendid civilisations, the Mycenaean, which flourished during the 2nd millennium* BC *and was influential throughout the then-known world, even as far as the South Wales coast.*

27. *The Lion Gate at Mycenae with its impressive relief, the oldest example of monumental sculpture in the West. The gate, the main entrance to the acropolis, and its opening was closed by a double door clad with sheets of bronze. The relief consists of two confronting lions, the heads of which were of different material attached by bronze connections, now missing. It is from these that the gate took its name and it is dated to circa 1250* BC.

28. *The Treasury of Atreus or Tomb of Agammemnon, the most impressive monumental building of the Mycenaean Age. The dromos, entrance to the tomb, which had a decorated entrance and the circular inner chamber with side room are preserved. The tomb's interior was also ornamented but its contents have not survived. It was constructed in 1250* BC.

26

Mycenaean Art

The art and civilisation which reached its zenith in Greece between 1600 and 1120 BC has been named "Mycenaean", since its fullest development was discovered at Mycenae. Some of the most representative, and also most impressive, examples of this art are the finds from the royal tombs of Grave Circle Ar. Objects of bronze, silver, electrum and principally of gold are so copious that they justify the city's fame as being "rich in gold". Weapons, pottery, tools and jewellery are distinguished by their decorative wealth, exceptional technique and fine workmanship constituting unique masterpieces. Outstanding are the gold mortuary masks, rings, cups and kylixes, decorative sheets of gold, sealstones and miniature carved objects, especially in ivory, as well as the swords, not only on account of the excellence of their execution and wealth of decoration, but also the variety of subjects. Mention should also be made of the grave stelae, figurines and wall paintings.

29. Gold face mask which belonged to some sovereign and which Schliemann attributed to Agamemnon. It was found in Grave Circle A.

30. Gold finger ring with representation of a cult scene, also from Grave Circle A.

31. Wall painting of the "Mycenaean lady" from the religious centre at Mycenae.

32. The Warriors' Krater from the homonymous house at Mycenae.

29

30

33

34

. The Theatre of Epidaurus, the best preserved ancient theatre, with excellent acoustics where musical and dramatic performances are still given. It was built within the area of the Sanctuary of Asklepios at the beginning of the 3rd century BC and, according to tradition, was the work of Polykleitos the younger. In the photograph one can see the circular orchestra, rows of seats, one of the entrances (parodoi) and the remains of the skene.

. The Mycenaean acropolis of Tiryns; aerial photograph. It was fortified with Cyclopean walls upon a low lock rising from the Argive Plain, just before Nauplion. The fortifications, remains of the palace on the top d the small gate are visible.

. Another view of the theatre of Epidaurus with part of the tiers and both parodoi.

Nauplion — Palamidi, Acronauplia, Bourtzi

36. The entrance to Palamidi, the fortress which dominates the town of Nauplion. Above the entrance is a relief of the lion of St. Mark, emblem of Venice.

37. Palamidi, as seen from the town of Nauplion. It was fortified for the first time by the Venetians in the 17th century and is connected to the lower, also fortified, hill of Acronauplia, by 857 steps, galleries and successive gates. Even today romantic visitors may climb the steep steps and enjoy the unique view from this fortress vantage point.

38. Acronauplia and part of the town of Nauplion, as seen from above. Nauplion has retained its old-world charm with its steep streets, Neoclassical houses and historic buildings. It was the first capital of the Greek State.

39. Bourtzi, the fortified islet of Aghioi Theodoroi which was linked to Acronauplia by a long chain which closed off the harbour. In recent times it was converted into an hotel, though this no longer operates.

36

37

44

40. *The Hodegetria monastery at Mystras, the now ruined Byzantine capital of the Palaeologues, which was built on a rocky eminence of the Taygetos mountains above Sparta. One may wander along its paved streets, visit churches with remarkable Byzantine wall paintings, see ruined houses and feel as if one is living in another age. On the very summit stands the castle, fortified by Guillaume Villehardouin in 1249, and a short distance below are the palaces.*

41. *The palace complex of the Despots of Mystras, as seen from above. Built in the main square of the Upper Town (Pano Polis), they comprise an impressive unity with the Palaeologue wing on the left and that of the Kantakuzenoi on the right.*

1

Art at Mystras

The monuments at Mystras, which was also capital of the Despotate founded after 1264, differ from all others in the Peloponnese, as well as from their contemporaries in Central Greece. The houses, palaces and churches built in this fortress-state are characterised by the diversity of their construction and high quality. Whoever wanders nowadays amidst the steep, narrow streets, the gates, the ruins of the houses, what has remained untouched by time, is astonished by the impressiveness of the landscape. The spirit and art of Mystras is preserved in its churches with their unique wall paintings, distinguished for their beauty, grace, expressiveness, diversity of themes and exceptional colouration and technique. In some of the wall paintings balance in composition and idealisation in the rendering of the figures still holds sway.

42. Angel with the Scroll. Wall painting from the narthex of the Metropolis at Mystras, detail from the Second Coming. Beginning of 14th century.

43. Martyrs, wall painting from the northwest side chapel in the Hodegetria (Aphentiko) church.

44. Entry to Jerusalem, wall painting from the Pantanassa church, circa 1430.

45. *Partial view of the island of Kythera south of the Peloponnese. The castle and a few brilliant white typical island houses can be seen.*

46. *The awe-inspiring crag of Monemvasia with traces of fortification on its summit. The town, with its fortifications and idiosyncratic architecture, nestles on the east side of the rock, where Byzantine churches and houses have survived, while the peak is crowned by the castle with its Byzantine church of Aghia Sophia.*

47. *Vatheia, one of the most typical villages of Mani with its tall towers. Mani is a region apart, both on account of its environment and architecture of its dwellings, and of its history and the independent character of its inhabitants.*

46

48. *The medieval castle of Methoni, as seen from above. On account of its advantageous location, Methoni played an important role in antiquity, when it acquired its first fortifications (4th century BC). In 1209 it was captured by the Venetians, who had coveted it for some time, and fortified a vast area. Today one enters the castle along the stone bridge over the moat and under an arched passageway into an immense space with imposing fortifications and gates. A large gate to the south leads to an octagonal tower, Bourtzi, built in 1500 to reinforce the fortress' defence. The modern town of Methoni extends to the north of the castle.*

49. *The town of Koroni with its ruined castle; aerial photograph. Also inhabited since antiquity, it too was taken by the Venetians who built its fortifications, just as in the corresponding castle at Methoni. Its location led to it being raided several times, like Methoni, and nowadays only a few ruins of its former impressive ramparts and buildings survive. Inside the castle there is the Monastery of the Precursor (Prodromos) which was built around the old Byzantine church of Aghia Sophia.*

50. *The harbour and picturesque town of Pylos with its two-storey houses and narrow streets leading up the hill slope. It preserves the atmosphere of an island town. It was here that, in 1827, the final blow was dealt to the Turko-Egyptian fleet, thus securing Greece's independence. In the right-hand corner of the photograph part of the castle of Niokastro is visible, which was built by the Turks in 1573 and is quite well preserved.*

48

51. The temple of Hera at Olympia with some of the restored columns. It dates from the 6th century BC and was the most sacrosanct spot in the Altis, the enclosed area with its sanctuaries, votives and installations for athletes who came to compete every four years on the occasion of the Panhellenic Olympic Games. It is from here that the sacred flame is taken in the modern Olympic Games and is held by young girls in chlamydes and chitons, as seen in the photograph.

52. The Palaestra, space intended for athletes to exercise, and for boxing and wrestling contests, was built in the area west of the Altis during the Hellenistic era and communicated directly with the Gymnasium, where the athletes also practised.

53. The temple of Apollo at Bassae, one of the best preserved ancient temples in Greece. It was built circa 420 BC, on top of an earlier temple, and dedicated to Apollo by the people of Phygaleia because he had saved them from plague. The temple, designed by Iktinos, is Doric, peripteral (6×15 columns) with pronaos, cella and opisthodomos and bore rich sculpted decoration of mythological subjects.

54

Art in the Olympia Museum

In the museum at Olympia, which is located close to the archaeological site, one can see artistic masterpieces either votives in the sanctuary or belonging to the decoration of the different buildings of the Altis. Vases, clay and bronze figurines, weapons, beaten sheets of metal and sculptures covering a time interval from the Neolithic age to the Roman era are displayed. These include sculptured compositions from the pediments and metopes of the temple of Zeus, the terracotta group of Zeus and Ganymede and, above all, the statue of Hermes with the Young Dionysos, work of Praxiteles, a unique creation of ancient art.

54. *The statue of Hermes with the young Dionysos. This famous statue, work of Praxiteles, is dated to circa 340 BC and is outstanding because of its expressiveness and perfection of execution.*

55. *Bronze sheet of the Archaic period (circa 630 BC) with hammered figures of Centaurs and a hoplite.*

56. *One of the most strongly expressive compositions from the sculptured decoration of the west pediment of the temple of Zeus, the subject of which is the Battle of Lapiths and Centaurs.*

57. Antirrhion, the promontory of Central Greece (Sterea Hellas) which, together with Rhion opposite, constitutes the west entrance to the Gulf of Corinth. In 1499 Bayazet II built two mighty castles here, Antirrhion or Molykrikon Rhion or of Roumeli (Sterea Hellas) and Rhion or of Morea (Peloponnese). Nowadays one passes from the Peloponnese to Sterea Hellas and towards Epirus via Rhion and Antirrhion. Beyond Antirrhion the road leads to Naupaktos.

5

58. *Partial view of Naupaktos and its harbour, as seen from the castle above. Naupaktos is a charming little town with a picturesque castle, the fortifications of which descend to and embrace the harbour. It is mainly Venetian, recalling the era when Naupaktos was known as Lepanto in the West. The coast road from Naupaktos passes through several pretty places; outstanding among them are Galaxeidi and Itea, from where one may ascend to Delphi.*

58

59

Delphi

59. *General view of the
site of Delphi which
was regarded as the
centre of the earth in
ancient times. Here
Apollo was
worshipped, the god of
light, music and, above
all, of prophecy, for
there was an oracle
which was consulted
from all over Greece
and the Orient. On the
hillslope one can see
the ruins of the
Sanctuary of Apollo,
the Stadium and
Theatre. Panhellenic
contests, musical and
athletic, the Pythian
Games, were held in
the stadium. The
modern visitor to the
sanctuary, like his
ancient counterpart,
follows the Sacred
Way leading between
the treasuries, votives
and bases of votives
and is introduced to
the unique atmosphere
created by the
extremely beautiful
landscape.*

60. The Tholos, the loveliest monument in the Sanctuary of Pronaia Athena, a short distance from the Delphic Sanctuary, on the bank overlooking the Pleistos valley. It was built at the beginning of the 4th century BC according to plans of the architect Theodoros. It is of Pentelic marble, circular in shape and had 20 columns all around its pteron. It bore rich sculpted decoration and with its correct proportions and finely worked details emanates architectural grace. Its function remains unknown.

61. Section of the Sacred Way with the Stoa and Treasury of the Athenians. The Treasuries were buildings dedicated by the cities to the Sanctuary of Apollo, in honour of the god. Many of them were adorned with rich sculpted decoration. The treasury of the Athenians was built at the end of the 6th century BC; parts of its reliefs are preserved in the museum of Delphi.

62. The temple of Apollo, the most significant edifice in the sanctuary, wherein the god was worshipped and the oracles delivered. The ruins belong to the 4th century BC temple which was Doric, peripteral (6×15 columns) with rich decoration on its pediments. On the tall pedestal, visible on the left, stood the equestrian statue of Prousias, king of Bithynia.

6

Art in the Delphi Museum

Here are housed treasures of great artistic value, both from the sanctuary of Apollo and that of Athena. Sculptures constitute by far the greatest number of exhibits, mainly coming from the decoration of edifices within the sanctuary, in particular the Treasuries of the Athenians and Siphnians. Mention should also be made of the colossal Naxian sphinx, the marble statues from the Votive of Daochos, the column with the dancing girls, the chryselephantine fragments from the large deposit near the Stoa of the Athenians and, finally, the world famous bronze statue of the Charioteer.

63. The famous bronze statue of the Charioteer, votive of Polyzalos, tyrant of Gela (circa 470 BC). It stood in the sanctuary of Apollo and comprised part of a large bronze group of sculptures. The strength, expressiveness, together with the calm and unrivalled technique of construction place it among the world's artistic masterpieces.

64. Ivory head with gold hair, probably representing Apollo.

65. Ivory head with gold diadem, most probably depicting Artemis. Both these heads are among the most impressive exhibits in the Delphi Museum.

66. Part of the north side of the frieze of the Siphnian Treasury, the subject of which is the Gigantomachy. 5th century BC.

63

Parnassos,
Hosios Loukas,
Arachova

*67. Parnassos, the
Gerondovrachos peak
with its winter-sports
centre to which many
ski enthusiasts flock.
The mountain was
sacred in antiquity to
Dionysos and the
Mainads. From here
one has a
spectacularly clear and
beautiful view. In
winter it is snow-clad
and there are several
ski runs.*

*68. The Monastery of
Hosios Loukas
Steiriotis, a few
kilometres before
Delphi. Located in a
delightful, tranquil
region, it constitutes
one of the most
interesting monastic
complexes with its two
churches (of the Virgin
and of Hosios
Loukas), cells,
refectory and crypt, in
which is the tomb of
the holy man. There
are wall paintings
dating from the 11th
century, as well as the
church of Hosios
Loukas renowned for
its mosaics and its
architectural plan.*

*69. The small,
amphitheatrical village
of Arachova, famed for
its woven goods, wine
and gurgling, flowing
waters. From here one
goes up to Parnassos.*

Eretria

70. *Chalkis and the Euripos Straits where the water changes direction every 6 or 7 hours.*

71-72 *Eretria, archaeological site and modern town in Euboia, the second largest Greek island, after Crete, which extends along the length of the coast of Attica and Boiotia. In antiquity it was one of the most important maritime cities with a school of philosophy and tradition in pottery making. After its destruction by the Romans (87 BC) it was not rebuilt. In the photograph one can see the West Gate, remains of the palace complex and the theatre, from where one ascends to the acropolis. Modern Eretria was built in 1824 by refugees from the island of Psara and most of it stands on the site of the ancient city.*

75

73. *View looking down on the town of Volos which is the commercial harbour of Thessaly. Behind the town looms Pelion, the mountain with its quaint villages and idyllic countryside which occupies the entire peninsula closing the Pagasitikos Bay. Pelion was considered by the ancient Greeks as the home of Cheiron, the wisest of the Centaurs, who looked after Jason and taught Achilles music.*

74. *The beach of Ai Yanni, one of the loveliest in Pelion. It is also the harbour of Kissos, the picturesque mountain village with its church of Aghia Marina which has interesting wall paintings.*

75. *Another typical Pelian village in its verdant setting and with its architecturally distinctive dwellings.*

76. *Partial view of the Plain of Thessaly, the most extensive in Greece, which is enclosed by high mountain ranges.*
77. *Part of the town of Larissa, built in the middle of the Plain of Thessaly on the right bank of*

the Peneios river. It is a bustling, modern town, yet has a very long history. Inside the town are preserved the remains of the Hellenistic theatre, ruins of a Classical temple, while on the low hill which was the ancient acropolis, stands the Clock Tower and, to the NE, the Byzantine fortress.

78. *Meteora, the town of Kalambaka and the village Kastraki. The high, precipitous rocks of Meteora, which suddenly rise from the Plain of Thessaly, are a phenomenon without equal in the world. Various opinions have been expressed concerning their formation. Some believe they were formed by the erosion of rocks, while others consider them to be cones of the delta of a river which, at the time when Thessaly was a lake, carried along rocks and boulders which aggregated to form a large cone which was then broken down into hills of different heights and shapes. Here anchorites and monks sought refuge and built small cells at first and, subsequently, created the great monasteries with their many treasures, notable ecclesiastical works, rich paintings and murals.*

79-80. *Two more views of the surrealistic rocks of Meteora. Of the 24 monasteries and host of hermitages which existed in older times, only 6 have survived: Metamorphosis or Megalo Meteoro, Barlaam, Aghios Stephanos, Aghios Nikolaos Anapausas, Aghia Triada, Rousanou and Hypapanti. Ruins of other monasteries and hermitages can be seen on the pinnacles of the sheer crags.*

7

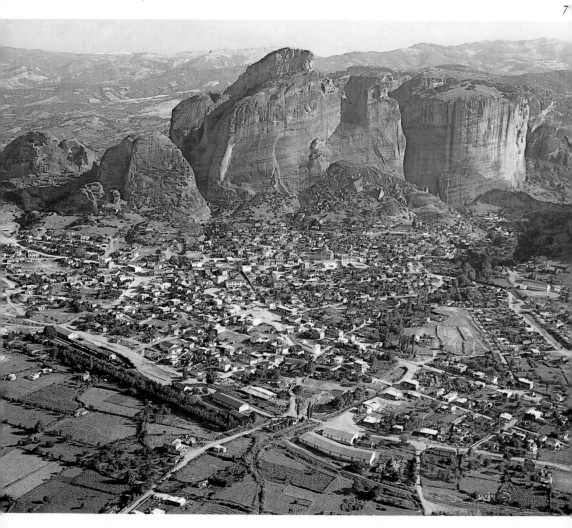

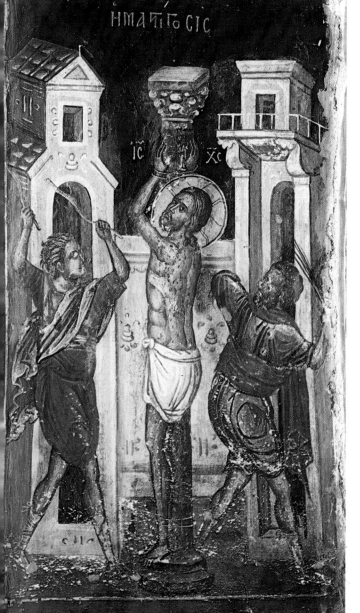

Art at Meteora

In the monasteries of Meteora Christian art developed, especially painting, furnishing us with some of the most splendid examples of Postbyzantine painting. This art was influenced by earlier prototypes and is distinguished by its light surfaces, simplicity and naturalness of its figures, expressive physiognomies and noble poses. Here are preserved the works of two great artists, Theophanes Strelitzas and Frangos Katellanos: the former is noted for his calm and formal style, the latter for his pronounced realism.

81. The Flagellation, wall painting from Aghios Nikolaos Anapausas.

82. Aghios Christophoros, 16th century wall painting from Aghios Nikolaos Anapausas.

83. Wall painting from Aghios Nikolaos Anapausas depicting an extremely rare subject, Adam naming the animals.

84. View of Tempe. The vale of Tempe is situated betwixt mounts Olympos and Ossa; through it flows the river Peneios. It is a region of incomparable natural beauty. The ancient Greeks attributed its formation to Poseidon and his earthquakes, though it was Apollo who was worshipped here. Tempe has been lauded by poets and writers throughout history on account of its exceptional landscape and idyllic environment.

85. Partial view of Olympos, the highest mountain in Greece, which rises between Thessaly and Macedonia. Its high peaks are snowcapped for most of the year, presenting a magnificent spectacle. Here the gods of the ancient Greek Dodekatheon had their home, fed on nectar and ambrosia and, indeed, one of its peaks, Stephani, was also called "Zeus' Throne". Nowadays the lower slopes are densely wooded, while the pine trees grow right up to the snow line.

86-87. Partial view of ancient Dion, beneath the northern slopes of Olympos, where Zeus and the Muses were worshipped. One can see the paved main street, the forum with small roofed theatre and remains of various buildings. The town plan in Roman times followed that of the Hellenistic predecessor. It was at Dion that the King Philip

86

II celebrated his victory after the capture of Olynthos and that Alexander the Great made a sacrifice before embarking on his campaign against the Persians. After the destruction wrought by the Goths under Alaric, the city never regained its former eminence.

Vergina

88. *Aerial photograph of the great tumulus of Vergina where the three royal tombs were discovered by Prof. Manolis Andronikos, in the centre of the small present-day village. The three tombs are covered by a roof. In the largest one, unplundered, objects of wondrous artistry in gold, silver, bronze and ivory, wall paintings with sensitive compositions and refined techniques, which constitute the most important examples of Hellenistic painting, were found. In the background is the cemetery of tumuli of the Geometric era.*

89. *The splendid Hellenistic palace at Vergina in its green, impressive setting at the foot of the slopes of the Pieria mountains. According to scholars, here was the site of Aigai, ancient capital of the kings of Macedon.*

Pella

90. *Aerial photograph of a house in ancient Pella, a typical example of a late 4th century BC residence in which the living quarters are arranged around a square peristyle courtyard.*

91. *Aerial photograph of ancient Pella, capital of the Macedonians since the beginning of the 4th century BC and a flourishing artistic centre. The painter Zeuxis is associated with Pella, as is the poet Agathon, who died here in 400 BC and the Tragic poet Euripedes (died 406 BC). Pella was the birthplace of Alexander the Great. Its prosperity is most clearly demonstrated by the wonderful mosaics of circa 300 BC discovered in the houses and which are nowadays exhibited in the museum, while others have been left 'in situ'. After 148 BC the region went into decline.*

91

Thessalonike

The walls
Arch of Galerius
Aghios Demetrios
White Tower

92. Section of the ramparts of Thessalonike, as they survive nowadays.

93. The Arch of Galerius and the Rotunda. This is a large triumphal arch built to commemorate the emperor Galerius' victory over the Persians in AD.297 Only a section of it has survived. On the same axis stands the Rotunda, which was built by Galerius to be used as his mausoleum. It soon became a church and, subsequently, a mosque.

94. The church of Aghios Demetrios, patron saint of Thessalonike. It is a large five-aisled basilica, the original nucleus of which dates from the 5th century.

95. View of the famous White Tower of Thessalonike. It was built about 1430 constituting part of the ramparts enclosing the city at the southern corner. From here one may admire the beautiful view, both over the Thermaic Gulf and over the city, which extends amphitheatrically on the slopes of Mount Chortiatis.

92

93

94

90

Thessalonike

96-97. *Views of the city of Thessalonike, the second largest in terms of population and importance in Greece and the centre of Northern Greece. The city has a very long history and was created by Kassandros in 316 BC by the unification of small conurbations with the initial settlement of Therme. It was named after the sister of Alexander the Great and soon fortified. Its development was rapid. During the reign of the emperor Justinian it was especially favoured and its influence continued in the*

years that followed, despite its being sacked and invaded several times. Today it is divided into the upper and lower town, where one may see significant Byzantine monuments side by side with modern highrise blocks. The unique treasures of the history of Macedonia are displayed in the archaeological museum. High up in Ano Polis (the upper town) are the Byzantine walls and within the acropolis area stands the Heptapyrgion, a fortress surmounted by seven towers.

97

The Art of Northern Greece in the Thessalonike Museum

Art in Northern Greece has a very long tradition, commencing in early Prehistoric times. A variety and abundance of Prehistoric finds is displayed in the Museum of Thessalonike, as well as finds from subsequent periods: Early Iron Age with finds from Vergina, pottery, weapons and jewellery, finds of the Classical period from Olynthos and a rich collection of sculptures from the Archaic to Roman era. There are also the wonderful treasures from Vergina, glass vases of the Roman period and mosaic floors, also of Roman times.

98. The famous gilded bronze krater of Derveni, work of the 4th century BC. It is decorated with relief figures of Satyrs and Mainads from the entourage of Dionysos and Ariadne. There are figures, in the round, from the Dionysiac company, on the shoulders, bearded figures on the volutes and relief animals on the neck.

99. Ivory head from Vergina in the form of a bearded man, depicting perhaps the king Philip II. It comes from the embellishment of the wooden bed in the great tomb at Vergina.

100. Large gold wreath of oak leaves, from the great tomb at Vergina.

101. Gold larnax from the great tomb at Vergina, decorated with the symbol of the Macedonian dynasty, the star, and floral motifs. It contained bones, perhaps of the king Philip II.

98

102. *View of the monastery of Dionysiou with its port. The monastery is built upon a precipitous cliff in the southwest of the Athos peninsula and some of its balconies are literally suspended above the sea. With its fortress-like architecture, the monastery has a forbidding appearance.*

103. *Part of the katholikon of the great monastery of Vatopedi with the Phiale and clock with the "negro". Vatopedi is located on the northeast side of the Athos peninsula, which is occupied by the monastic state of the Holy Mountain or Mt. Athos, with its monasteries, with their countless treasures, hermitages and places of retreat. The monastery churches (katholika) house many works of art, wall paintings, icons and treasures of inestimable value. There are twenty large monasteries in the interior and on the coast of the peninsula, where the institution of "abaton" is observed, i.e. approach is forbidden to all females. The peninsula is the easternmost promontory of the large Chalkidike peninsula, situated between the Strymon and the Thermaic gulfs comprising three prongs with extremely beautiful idyllic countryside.*

104. The aqueduct of the monastery of Stavronikita with the defensive tower in the background. This monastery is built in the middle of the northeast side of the peninsula on top of a rock and its katholikon is the smallest on Mt. Athos.

105. The monastery of Xenophontos as seen from the sea. It is built on a smooth eminence on the east side of the peninsula.

105

The Art of Mount Athos

On Mount Athos Byzantine art is represented by a host of excellent quality works, both in architecture, painting and miniature art. In painting, in particular, a tradition was created which continues even today, with works of high technical and aesthetic merit. Wall paintings, portable icons, miniatures in manuscripts constitute diverse manifestations of painting. This art is influenced by artistic trends outside Athos. The first wall paintings are dated to the 12th century, while the zenith was achieved during the 14th-16th century, when we have wall paintings with light colours, realistic faces, agility and naturalness, together with the metaphysical dimension. The decoration of the illuminated manuscripts is also rich and multi-coloured. The majority are artistic masterpieces.

106. Marginal miniature in a menologion from the monastery of Esphigmenou. It is dated to the 11th century and depicts a bucolic scene.

107. Reliquary of Aghios Nephon, from the monastery of Dionysiou. It is in the shape of a church and is dated to the 16th century. Many treasures are housed on Mt. Athos.

108. Wall painting from the monastery of Megisti Lavra, dated to the 19th century and depicting the Parable of the Prodigal Son.

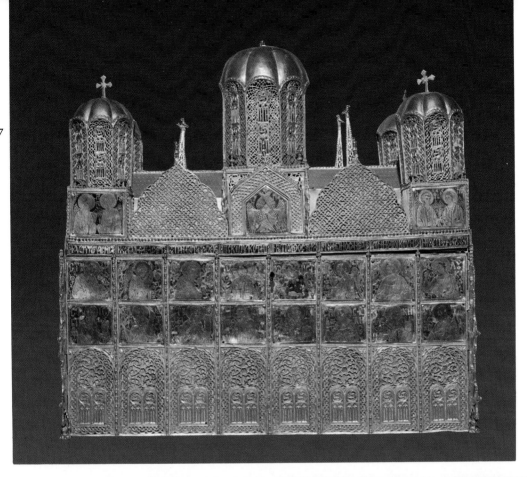

Philippi

109. *View of the forum at Philippi. The city took its name from king Philip II of Macedonia who captured it in 356 BC. Its importance grew with the construction of the Via Egnatia as a military road. It was here that, in 42 BC, the famous battle was waged against Caesar's assassins. At Philippi St. Paul preached the Gospel for the first time on European soil in AD 49. The excavated area extends to right and left of the modern road: on the left is the large Roman forum and on the right the ruins of the theatre, the Basilica A and, at the top, the acropolis crowned by medieval fortifications. A short distance from Basilica A was a Roman crypt, considered to be the place where St. Paul was incarcerated and later painted with scenes from his life. A chapel was built on top of it. The forum is a large paved area with stoas on three sides, accessible via steps and*

109

with a bema, fountains, two temples, library and houses from the time of Augustus. To the south are the ruins of Basilica B.

110. Basilica B at Philippi. Building of the church commenced in the 6th century AD and material from the Roman palaestra and a covered market place was used in its construction. The basilica did not have the appearance intended by the architect because the north wall collapsed. After the invasion of the Bulgars in 837 the west one fell down too, while the still-standing narthex was converted into a small church in the 10th century. Nowadays, in the ruins which have remained, the pillars with the acanthus-leaf decoration on the capitals are of interest.

10

Kavala

111. General view of Kavala. The city occupies the site of ancient Neapolis which was the harbour of Philippi and the main port of disembarkation for those travelling to Europe from the East. St. Paul disembarked here. In Byzantine times it was named Christoupolis. Ancient remains of the sanctuary of Parthenos and of the ancient city wall have been revealed. Most of the monuments are Byzantine and medieval. Apart from the fortress there is an aqueduct (16th century) and the Imaret, one of the most important Turkish buildings. Interesting local finds are exhibited in the museum of the town.

11

112. View of the town of Kavala with its castle, built on top of the promontory. Kavala is the second largest city of Macedonia, built amphitheatrically around the gulf, and is a good base for getting to know the surrounding region and, in particular, Philippi. The castle stands on a promontory to the east, occupying the site of the ancient acropolis. The walls, in which ancient material has been incorporated, are of the Byzantine era and were repaired in 926, after an earthquake, and again in the 16th century. Here also is the house in which Mehmet Ali, future Pasha of Egypt.

Thasos

113. *View of the island of Thasos, the northernmost island of the Aegean with an age-old history. A colony of Paros, it achieved its zenith at the end of the 6th and beginning of the 5th century BC. The present capital of the island, Limani, stands on the site of the ancient city. Excavations have brought to light many of the ancient buildings and the defensive enclosure of the walls, which had several towers, turrets and gates. The acropolis was located on the hill, while the ancient city occupied an extensive area around it. Ancient buildings are encountered here and there, both in the present town and the environs of the island of Thasos. One of the most important is the ancient theatre which was first built in the 4th century BC and in Roman times was rearranged for staging struggles with wild beasts. It is set in the heart of a wood of oak and pine trees. Upon the acropolis are the ramparts built by the Genoese, as well as other ancient remains, traces of ancient temples and edifices and the area of the agora. The finds exhibited in the local museum include exceptional examples of ancient art.*

113

114-115. Thasos has extremely beautiful, lushly verdant countryside, some of the loveliest in the Aegean, and picturesque hamlets. Among them is Limenaria, on the southwest coast, most modern of the ten villages of the island. Thasos has plenty of forests with pines, planes and chestnut trees, while in coastal places tobacco and olives are cultivated. On the island mineral and marble quarries, famous in antiquity, still work.

116 and 119. Two views of the town of Kastoria, built on a pleasant site on the isthmus of a small peninsula of the homonymous lake. Most of its inhabitants are involved in the processing and making of fur garments. The town was thus named in Byzantine times, to which period part of the ramparts, preserved close to the neck of the isthmus, date. One of its most idyllic spots is the lakeside from where one has a unique view over the surrounding mountains and the lake, on the shores of which birds usually gather and wade.

117. Kastoria has lovely two-storeyed mansions, dating from the 17th and 18th century, set amidst trees and narrow cobbled streets.

118. Churches abound in the town of Kastoria. Seven of them are of the Byzantine era, while the rest are postbyzantine or medieval. Of the total of 72 which the town is said to have had, only 54 have remained. The majority are of the basilica type with external decorative brickwork, while the interiors have wall paintings. Some of the outside walls of the churches also bear murals.

116

119

118

120. *The entrance to the municipal museum in the castle (Aslam mosque) with its heaps of cannon balls. Among the most impressive exhibits are the 18th and 19th century jewellery and costumes of Epirus.*

121. *View of the lake and town of Ioannina. Capital of Epirus, Ioannina is built on the shore of lake Pamvotis, amidst dark green mountains. Small craft ply between the town and the picturesque island in the lake, on which there are several noteworthy monasteries. Ioannina combines a semblance of modernity with the numerous extant elements of its historic past, days when it was renowned for its gold-work, woven fabrics and woodcarving. A few kilometres away, to the north of the lake, is the Perama cave with its intricate stalagmite and stalactite decoration, one of the most spectacular in Europe.*

121

Pindos

122. View of Pindos. The Pindos mountains, offshoot of the Dinaric Alps, run through mainland Greece from north to south, separating Thessaly from Epirus. Its highest peaks are to the east and southeast of Ioannina and its slopes are thickly wooded with oak, pine and fir trees. Some of Greece's major rivers have their source in Pindos. Wild animals still roam free in many parts.

122

123. Villagers of Metsovo dance attired in their local costumes. Metsovo is built high up in the Pindos, in an impressive verdant environment. It is famed for its folk art, handicraft and cottage industries (woven goods, embroideries, woodcarving) and elaborate traditional costumes, which the villagers still wear, especially on feast days. In the restored "archontiko" of M. Tositsa are exhibited beautiful local handicrafts.

123

124

125

124. View of the archaeological site of Nikopolis, near Preveza. Several of the Roman buildings have survived from the city built by Augustus after his victory at Actium; the theatre, the stadium, remains of the aqueduct which brought water from the river Louros, sections of the walls, one of the gates and the restored Roman odeum, in which performances are given during the annual festival. There are also Early Christian basilicas.

125. The ancient theatre of Dodona, built in the reign of Pyrrhus (297-272 BC) and later destroyed and rebuilt. In Roman times alterations were made so that it could be used as an arena. The theatre is nowadays restored and performances of ancient drama are given every year.

126. The famous bridge of Arta, immortalised in popular legend, which was built over the river Arachthos at the exit from the town, in the 17th century.

127. The bridge of "Kokori" in the Zagori region, with the so-called Davelis cave.

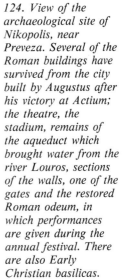

115

128. View of Parga, one of the most enchanting towns in Greece. Built around a small gulf opposite the island of Paxoi, it has superb sandy beaches. The town stands on a rocky promontory dominated by the massive castle still adorned with the Lion of St. Mark, even though the fortress is Norman. From Parga one can visit the river Acheron, site of the famous necromanteion of Ephyra, one of the most renowned in antiquity, where the oracles were pronounced by the dead. It was also a sanctuary of Pluto and Persephone and one of the gates of Hades for the ancient Greeks.

129. Igoumenitsa, another of the towns of Epirus and principal harbour for communication with Corfu and Italy.

Ionian isles - *Corfu*

130. The church of
Aghios Spyridon in
Corfu, built in 1590 in
honour of the patron
saint of the island. The
saint's relics are
preserved in a splendid
reliquary which is kept
inside the sanctuary
and is taken in
procession four times a
year, when masses are
celebrated to
comemmorate the
saint's miracles, which
saved the island from
epidemics and
catastrophes.

131. One of Corfu's
outstanding landscapes
is the region of Kanoni
with the two
enchanting islets at its
southern extremity.
The first, with the
church of Vlacherna,
is linked by a narrow
strip to the mainland
opposite; the second,
Pontikonisi, drowned
in greenery with the
church of the
Pantocrator, presents a
picture of
incomparable beauty.

132. View of
Palaiokastritsa, one of
the most captivating
shores of Corfu, with
its picturesque bays,
impressive cliffs and
vibrant hues of blue
and green. It was here
that king Alkinoos
entertained Odysseus
in his palace, whose
ship is said to have
been petrified and is
today a rock a little
way offshore.

133. View of Ithaka, the small remote island which was the home of Homer's Odysseus. Despite its mountainous terrain, there are many anchorages and bays (Homeric "limenes panormoi"), as well as small fertile valleys and plains. Its capital, Vathy, is situated in the recess of a gulf which separated the island into two parts.

134-135. Two views of the island of Lefkas with its tranquil landscape and picturesque bays, separated by a small channel from the opposite shore of Aitoloakarnania. The island has a very long history, evidence of which has been found at Nydri and the finds are housed in the local museum. The most impressive monument on Lefkas is the medieval fortress of Santa Maura. In the south part of the island is cape Lefkatas, where there was a temple of Apollo. Here, in antiquity, the famous practice of immersion of those wishing to be cured of unrequited love took place.
It is from here that the ancient poetess Sappho is said to have leapt into the sea.

Kephalonia

136. Partial view of Kephalonia with the village of Assos, one of the island's beauty spots. Betwixt vineyards, mountains and sea, stand quaint houses and imposing villas. The mass of the ruined Venetian castle dominates the village from above.

137-138. Two views of the island of Kephalonia, the largest of the Ionian islands. The island was named after the Athenian Kephalos, who came and settled there. Many ancient remains are preserved on the island, the most important being those of the Mycenaean cemetery near the village of Mazarakata. Sights on the island include the cave of Melissane one of the most important in Greece. The island's features are its rich vegetation, fortresses, monasteries, picturesque towns and villages, as well as the fantastic colours of its sea.

7

8

139. *View of the town of Zakynthos with the Solomos museum and part of the castle in the background. Zakynthos has a rich poetic and musical tradition and was the home of two great Greek poets, A. Kalvos and the national poet, D. Solomos. Their mausoleum stands in Solomos Square, along with the museum housing personal effects of the latter, as well as memorabilia of the history of the Ionian islands and some icons.*

139

140

140. *View of the harbour of Zakynthos with the castle high on the hill. Although rebuilt after the catastrophic earthquakes of 1953, the town of Zakynthos retains its markedly traditional element. Some of its famous churches and mansions have been repaired, while others have been lost forever. On the south shore of the harbour stands the basilica of Aghios Dionysios, with the relics of the island's patron saint.*

141-142. Two views of Myrina, the capital of the island of Lemnos. The town is dominated by the imposing mass of the Venetian castle which was built on the site of the ancient acropolis, where there was a temple of Artemis. The fortress was repaired when the Turks occupied the island, but the ancient remains are visible at many points along the walls.

141

143. View of Mytilene, capital of the island of Lesbos. Atop the hill (in the background) is the castle, from where one has a superb view of the town and the shores of Asia Minor opposite. The castle was built by the Genoese on top of the preceding Byzantine one, on the same site as the acropolis stood in antiquity. The Turks built a Medresé, theological school, within the castle. Opposite the castle are the ruins of the ancient theatre, to the north of it are preserved sections of a 5th century polygonal wall, while at a lower level there are the ruins of a Roman villa in which were found wonderful mosaics of the 4th century, with scenes from the comedies of Menander. Mytilene has a museum, and an art gallery with works by the folk artist Theophilos.

144. Partial view of Methymna, the most typical village of Lesbos and one of the most astonishingly beautiful in Greece. It is built amphitheatrically, with a Genoese castle at the top of the hill, built by the Gatelouzoi and from where there is a fantastic view.

145. Yet another view of Methymna, also known as Molyvos. This coastal village of Lesbos is built to an irregular plan and its houses have an entirely different appearance, endowing them with particular quaintness and colour. Every year many intellectuals and artists flock to Molyvos.

14

144

145

Samos

146. The column from the sanctuary of Hera (Heraion) on Samos. The sanctuary is situated on the coast, a few kilometres outside the town of ancient Samos (nowadays Pythagoreion) and is called Kolona, on account of the sole surviving column of the temple. The temple of Hera was one of the largest of its age. It was built in the middle of the 6th century BC but was destroyed quite soon after by conflagration. Later, construction of a new temple commenced, but it was never completed. It is from this second temple that the extant column originates. Preserved in the Heraion are remains of Roman temples, altars, an Archaic and a Hellenistic stoa, an Early Christian basilica and even Mycenaean traces.

147-148. Two views of Pythagoreion, located in the south of the island. It is built in the region of ancient Samos and a section of the ramparts has survived, as well as ruins of the ancient theatre. Of particular interest is the Eupalineion tunnel which supplied ancient Samos with water and was completed in the days of Polykrates, c. 524 BC.

149

150

149. View of the village of Vrontados on Chios. North of the village is Daskalopetra, the so-called stone of Homer, which was probably connected with some shrine for a local cult. The island is considered to be one of the places sought as the home of Homer, the great epic poet. There are monuments throughout the island, from antiquity to the recent past. One of the most important places is Nea Moni, with its Byzantine monastery and 11th century church decorated with excellent mosaics. There are traditional medieval villages on the island, Mesta, Olympoi and Pyrgi.

150. Pyrgi, on Chios, a small medieval village in the south of the island. One can visit the medieval fortress and numerous churches, most of which have wall paintings as well as the distinctive streets with the arches. The exterior of many Pyrgian houses is also impressive, decorated in an original manner.

151. View of the small island of Psara.

152. View of the tiny island of Oinouses with its many mansions and churches.

133

153-155. *Picturesque landscapes and shores of the cosmopolitan island of Skiathos. The island has rich vegetation and many beaches, outstanding among them being that at Koukounaries (above right) where the pine trees embrace the sand. The beach at Lalaria (below right) is also wonderful with its pierced rock, an ideal place for swimming and water sports.*

153

Skopelos

156. View of the picturesque island of Skopelos whose ancient inhabitants came from Crete, led by the coloniser Staphylos, whose tomb has been found here. The island has a beautiful coastline and cool summer resorts.

157. Another view of Skopelos, Glossa, which is also the island's second harbour and marvellous summer resort, thanks to the refreshing breeze.

158. Chora, on Skopelos, with its brilliant white houses, many of which still retain their traditional grey-blue slate roofs. Chora has countless churches and several monasteries, as is true for the island as a whole, which is also renowned for its elaborate female costumes.

156

58

Alonissos

159-161. Three views of the island of Alonissos, also known by its Byzantine name of Liadromia or Lidromia. In antiquity it was called Ikos and ruins have been found on the east side of the island in the locality of Kokkinokastro.

159

Skyros

162. The harbour of Skyros, Linaria, located about the middle of the west side of the island, opposite Euboea with which it is connected by ferry-boat.

163. View of a picturesque Skyros beach, Magazia, below Chora.

164. View of Chora, Skyros, seen from above. The village is built amphitheatrically on the slope of a high hill and is dominated by the fortifications of its castle, which was built by the Byzantines and subsequently reinforced by the Venetians. In the walls of the castle traces of ancient material can be observed, while above the gate there is the Lion of St. Mark. The Byzantine monastery of Aghios Georgios (founded 962), famed for its miracles, stands within. Skyros is characterised by its stark white cuboid houses, steep narrow streets, wonderful embroideries, costumes, peculiar customs and its lively festivals. Beautiful multicoloured ceramics with genuine folk motifs are still made on Skyros. It is also renowned for its ponies. The island has a rich history and mythological tradition and it is said that Achilles hid here, among the daughters of king Lykomedes, and was then discovered by Odysseus.

162

Cyclades -*Syros*

165. *View of Hermoupolis, capital of Syros and also of the Nome (county) of the Cyclades. It is distinguished by its noble aspect with its many Neoclassical houses and public buildings, testifying to its illustrious and affluent past. Ano Syros, to the northwest, is completely medieval in character and was exclusively inhabited by Catholics in days gone by. It is built on the mountain slope and on the summit stands the Catholic church of San Giorgio, built in the 12th century, as well as the monastery of the Capuchins. Opposite is the Orthodox church of the Resurrection. In antiquity the island was one of the centres of the Cycladic civilisation and at Chalandriani graves of this era have been found.*

166. *View of Phoinikas the loveliest beach on the island.*

167. *Vari, another beach on Syros, one of the most sheltered on the island.*

165

168. *Partial view of Chora, Tinos with the monastery of Evangelistria. In antiquity Tinos was called Hydrousa and Ophiousa. It is known as the island of the Virgin (Panaghia) and is filled with terraced fields, lushly verdant regions, countless churches and villages with a Cycladic, yet medieval colour. The island is still known for its marble and its experienced marble-carvers, as well as for the architecture of its dovecotes, dating from the time of the Venetian occupation of the island.*

169. *Ktikados, one of the villages of Tinos.*

170. *The Monastery of Panaghia Evangelistria built on the spot where the miraculous icon of the Virgin was found in 1822, after a vision of the nun Pelagia. The white marble church, built on a vantage point dominating Chora, is a place of pilgrimage for all Orthodoxy. Next to it is the Art Gallery in which are displayed works by Greek and local artists, while in the museum are exhibited finds from the ancient temple of Poseidon and Amphitrite.*

Andros

171-173. *Three views of the island of Andros, the second largest of the Cyclades. In marked contrast to the rest of the Cyclades, Andros is well-wooded, mainly with pine trees. The island has plenty of water, which is why it was called Hydrousa in antiquity, and has natural therapeutic springs. Medieval monuments abound on Andros and in the capital, Chora (top right) there are impressive buildings, ancient remains and an interesting museum. The most important harbour is Gavrion, a summer resort, as are Batsi, Korthion and Apikia with the Sariza mineral springs.*

1

Mykonos

174. View of the harbour of Mykonos, the most frequented Cycladic island with its little white houses, narrow streets, chapels and bright white windmills. It retains all its Cycladic charm and beauty and has a constant stream of visitors, particularly during the summer, on account of the island's international reputation.

175-176. Two views of Mykonos with graphic details, characteristic of island life, especially during the summer months. The dazzling whiteness of the houses contrasts sharply with the colourful throng and azure sky.

174

177. *View of the archaeological site of Delos. The island, which was a religious and political centre in antiquity, birthplace of Apollo and Artemis, is today a vast, uninhabited archaeological site. Excavations have revealed the principal buildings and areas of the island: the great sanctuary of Apollo, panhellenic centre in antiquity, the area of the Sacred Lake, the commercial quarter and harbour with its moles, quays, shops and a 3rd century BC city, which may be compared with that at Pompeii. There are other sanctuaries, shrines and votives. To the west of the Sacred Lake was the famous Terrace of the Lions, carved in Naxian marble in the 7th century BC. There were nine lions in all, guardians of the sacred area; nowadays five remain. One was conveyed to Venice in the 17th century, where it still adorns the arsenal.*

178. *In the photograph we see part of the small sanctuary of Dionysos, distinguished by its many choregic monuments in the form of phalli. One has Dionysiac scenes on the base. They were erected circa 300 BC.*

179. *The marble facade of the restored temple of Isis. At the far end of the cella is the goddess' statue.*

Delos

180. Mosaic floor from the House of the Masks on Delos. It was found in the courtyard, since houses of the Hellenistic and Roman era were built around a central atrium with mosaic floor which covered the cistern in which the rain water was stored. With outstanding expressiveness and use of colour, Dionysos is depicted seated on a panther, holding a thyrsus and crowned with a wreath of vine leaves.

181. Mosaic floor from the House of the Masks.

182. Mosaic floor with a representation of a Panathenaic amphora, from the House of the Trident.

183. Mosaic floor from the House of the Dolphins.

180

182

184. View of Paroikia, capital of Paros. The isle belongs to the central Cyclades and is characterised by its mild climate and beautiful beaches. Home of the ancient lyric poet Archilochos, it is famed for its marble, as well as for its Postbyzantine churches and monasteries. One of the most important monuments is the Byzantine church of Panaghia Katapoliani. In the photograph one can see part of the Venetian castle with the church of Aghios Konstantinos.

185-186. Kolymbithres with its peculiar rock formations, in the village of Naoussa, one of the loveliest landscapes on the island with a superb beach.

187. Another coastal village and fishing spot on Paros, Piso Leivadi.

184

186

Naxos

188-189. Two views of
Chora, Naxos. The mass of
the Venetian castle is visible
in the centre and at the left
edge above the portal of the
Archaic temple of Apollo (6th
century BC). Naxos is the
largest island in the Cyclades
and on it are preserved
monuments from antiquity, as
well as from the era of the
Venetian occupation. There
are also several Byzantine
and Postbyzantine churches
and traditional mountain
villages.

188

Ios

190-193. Views of Ios, a small Cycladic island lying between Paros and Santorini with beautiful landscape, picturesque shores, typical Cycladic churches, houses and windmills. The capital is built on top of the ancient city, while the ruins of the 15th century Venetian castle are also preserved. According to tradition, the poet Homer was buried on Ios when his boat sank on a voyage from Samos to Athens. His alleged tomb is at Plakoto.

93

Santorini

194. View of Santorini with its harbour, tortuous stepped ascent, part of Phera, the island's capital. The volcanic isle of Santorini (Thera) attracts considerable attention among the Cyclades, on account of the excavations here which have revealed an entire city with its houses and streets, as well as its finds, which are among the most significant of the Cycladic civilisation.

195-196. Two views of Phera with its delightful houses, churches, unusual environment which charms and surprises one. Kato Phera (below right) is the most characteristic quarter with steep, narrow streets, houses, many of which still keep their vaulted roofs, and its churches. The white of the houses and the blue of the sea are combined in a unique composition.

95

Wall paintings of Thera

A quite distinct expression of Cycladic art are the wall paintings originating on Santorini *(Thera),* some of the oldest examples of monumental painting in Greece. The wall paintings fascinate not only because of their thematic wealth, variety of colours and vitality, but also because of the artist's ability to dominate space and handle it in a unique manner. The wall painting of the Ladies, the miniature fresco of the naval campaign, the wall painting with the Monkeys, of the Young Priestess, the Fisherman, the Boxing Children and of the Antelopes are a few of the best-preserved and most typical brought to light in the excavations. They are also an invaluable source of information about life on the island at the end of the 16th century BC. The most wonderful of all is that of Spring, with its delicate lilies, rocks and swallows, which exude fine grace and vital loveliness.

197. The Fisherman fresco, one of the best preserved.

198. The wall painting of the Boxing Children, showing two children boxing with cheerful disposition yet seriousness.

199. The wall painting of the Young Priestess, in which the markedly Minoan influence on the artist is discernible.

Melos

200-202. *Melos, one of the most interesting islands of the Cyclades, as much for its countryside as for its monuments and its history. The island is distinguished for its natural beauty, delightful beaches, as are the nearby islets of Antimelos and Glaronisia; the latter with their peculiar rock composition and formations constitute a unique phenomenon. Melos is also known for its Early Christian catacombs, the famous statue of Aphrodite, found on the site of Klima where there are ancient ruins and mainly, however, for Phylakopi, the ancient site where excavations have brought to light a city with three successive settlement phases, very important finds and interesting wall paintings. The island's main harbour is Adamas, from where one wends ones' way up to the capital, Plaka which is dominated by its Venetian castle, apparently occupying the site of the ancient acropolis. Also uniquely quaint is the hamlet of Kastro, beyond Plaka, with its now ruined Venetian castle and arched main entrance.*

200

Siphnos

203-204. *Two views of Siphnos, an island in the west Cyclades which preserves its authentic island architecture virtually intact, both in its capital, Apollonia and in Artemonas and the other hill villages. The old capital of the island, Kastro, is built on a precipitous conical hill on the east coast, on the site of ancient Siphnos, remains of which have survived. The village is dominated by the Venetian dastle and has a distinctive "couleur local".*

205. *Like the other isles of the Cyclades, Siphnos has many churches including that of Panaghia Chrysopigi on the southwest side of the island, which is associated with many local traditions. Nearby there are lovely bays and beaches, as well as the villages where traditional Siphnian pottery is still made. This side of the island is more easily accessible from the sea than from the hinterland.*

205

Kea

206. *View of Chora, Kea from afar. It is built upon a hill in the island's interior, amphitheatrically with tall houses which preserve their distinctive Cycladic architecture. It is divided into Pano and Kato (Upper and Lower) Chora and is a particularly attractive island town with its steep narrow streets and covered archways. The museum houses notable finds, testimonies of the island's long history.*

207. *View of Chora, Kea, the closest Cycladic island to Attica. Chora is built on the site of ancient Ioulis and its northwest side is dominated by the now ruined medieval castle. Above its central gate is the coat-of-arms of the Pangalos family.*

208. *Kea (Tzia) has lovely coves and beaches, such as this one at Otzia. A short distance before, in the vicinity of Vourkari, is the prehistoric settlement of Aghia Irini, where excavations have revealed finds of great significance. Kea was evidently settled from very early times (Bronze Age). At Korisia (present day Livadi and central harbour of the island) ruins of the temple of Apollo have been found, while at the southeast edge of the island are preserved the ruins of ancient Karthaia. At Aghia Marina one can see the ruins of a large Hellenistic tower surrounded by the now ruined monastery of Aghia Marina.*

Cycladic Civilisation

In the Cyclades, from the end of the 3rd millennium BC there developed a distinctive, yet uniform culture, independent of other contemporary ones. The principal artistic expression of the Cycladic civilisation are the Cycladic figurines. The majority are female, quite bewitching with their plastic perfection and expressiveness, as well as their individuality in the rendering of personal details.

In addition to figurines the Cycladic islanders made vases, jewellery, weapons and clay vessels, while a separate category of art creations are the wall paintings.

209. Marble figurine of a flute player from the deserted island of Keros, opposite Amorgos. He holds two flutes in his hand. This is one of the rare male Cycladic figurines and at the same time one of the most wonderful and lauded.

210. Marble figurine of a harpist from Keros. One of the most astounding Cycladic figurines on account of its expressiveness, the excellence of its chiselling and indication of all dimensions.

3908

Dodecanese - *Rhodes*

211. *View of Mandraki, the harbour of Rhodes with the deer at its entrance. Rhodes, thanks to its wonderful climate, long history and numerous monuments, ancient and medieval, its distinctive atmosphere, is today one of the best-known touristic islands. Wealthy and powerful in antiquity, it was the focus of interest and, therefore one of the most densely populated regions with centres under its influence (Lindos, Kamiros, Ialysos) and intense cultural, commercial and political activity. Nowadays one can see monuments from the era when Rhodes was occupied by the Knights of St. John.*

212. *View of Rhodes with the Grand Master's palace, on the north side of the Old Town, which was in fact a second fortress within the fortified town.*

213. *View of Lindos with its famous acropolis, the picturesque village and harbour. Built on the east side of the island, Lindos is one of the most impressive landscapes in Greece. On its unique acropolis one can see both Hellenistic and medieval monuments. The medieval houses in the village are also wonderful, with pleasing proportions and elegant decorations. Lindos is also famous for its outstanding ceramics.*

2

214

Rhodian Art

There was considerable artistic activity in Rhodes, examples of which can be seen on display in its museum and which cover a time span from the Mycenaean to the Roman period. Its artistic tradition continued even into more recent times, as can be seen in the island's folk museum. The great development in art began in the middle of the 5th century BC when a host of artists flocked to the island. Among the masterpieces of Rhodian art are the Victory (Nike) of Samothrace (Louvre), dedicated by the Rhodians in the sanctuary of the Kabeiroi, following their victory over Antiochus II in 190 BC, as well as the sculpted group of Laokoön (Vatican), work of the middle of the 2nd century BC.

214. Marble statue of Aphrodite bathing, copy of an original work by Doidalsas. 1st century BC.

215. Marble head of Helios, one of the best examples of Rhodian art of the 2nd century BC.

216. Clay female bust. Dated to the first half of the 5th century BC. Traces of colour are preserved.

217. Rhodian vase of the "Phikeloura" type with decoration influenced by eastern prototypes. 6th century BC.

218. Rhodian oinochoe of the 7th century BC, decorated with animals.

215

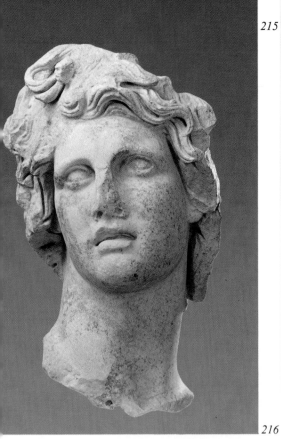

216

217

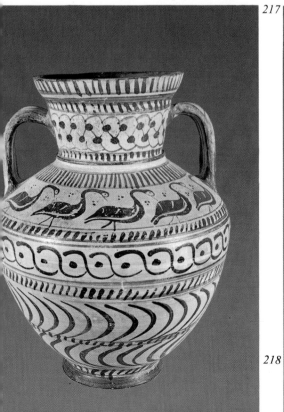

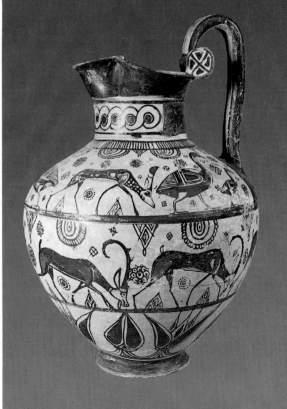

218

219. *The Asklepieion in Kos, which is situated a short distance from the town in a magnificent landscape. Of the sanctuary one can see part of the Doric temple of Asklepios (columns and foundations), an altar, architectural members from a Roman temple and ruins of the Stoa which housed Hippokrates' medical school.*

220. *Part of the medieval castle at the edge of the harbour. It is in a good state of preservation and constitutes a classic example of defensive architecture of the 15th century.*

219

221. The Roman odeum with its tiers of seats, one of the best-preserved buildings of the ancient city. From its 14 marble rows of seats, only seven are original

222. View of the town of Kos, the largest, after Rhodes, in the Dodecanese. Home of Hippokrates and of the 4th century painter Apelles it has had a turbulent history, commencing in the Neolithic era. The island is rich in monuments and in natural beauty, life is quiet and Kos attracts many visitors.

221

223. *Part of the fortified monastery of St. John on Patmos which dominates the centre of Chora by its sheer massiveness. It was founded in 1088 by the monk Christodoulos under the patronage and with bequests of the emperor Alexios I Comnenos. In its sacristy are stored many treasures of great value. Between Chora and Skala is the Grotto of the Apocalypse, where the exiled John the Evangelist wrote his Revelation. (The Chapel of the Holy Cross and the flat roofs of the Monastery, looking east).*

224. *View of Patmos. The island has kept its ancient name and is nowadays a place of pilgrimage. The island experienced a period of prosperity in the 16th century, when its inhabitants excelled as seafarers. Even today there is evidence of the wealth thus accrued.*

225. *View of Chora with the fortified monastery. Chora is built on the slopes of a hill and has a marvellous view. With its mansions, narrow streets, and courtyards of its authentic traditional houses it is a poem of folk architecture and a uniquely beautiful island town. The massive fortified monastery imparts a mysterious atmosphere and especial charm.*

Symi

226-227. *Two views of the island of Symi, also known as the island of Panormitis, after the famous monastery dedicated to the Taxiarch Michael. The island has very beautiful countryside. Its capital, Symi, built amphitheatrically on the slopes of a mountain, has fine two-storeyed houses which rise up as far as the castle of the Knights. The painted house façades in Ano Symi are painted in two colours, giving the erroneous impression that they are two separate houses. The island's harbour is full of life and movement, especially during the summer months, as more and more people discover its unique charm.*

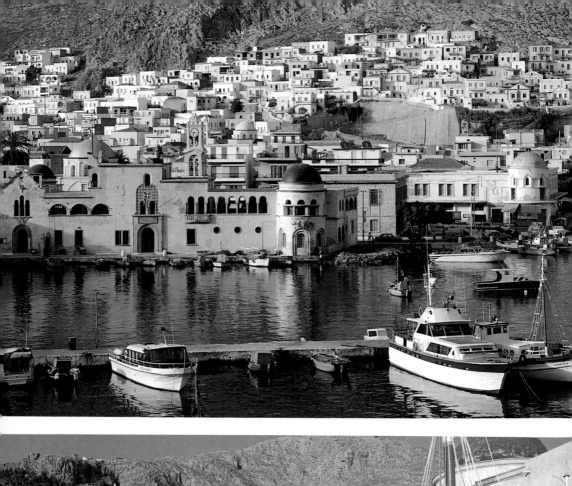

Kalymnos

228-230. Kalymnos, isle of the sponge-divers, one of the most interesting in the Dodecanese. Its capital, Pothia, is built around a bay on the south side of the island and is its commercial and seafaring centre. From here the sponge-divers depart for the northern shores of Africa, immediately after Easter, and the island goes into a torpor until the autumn, when they return. There are many monuments of the island's history. Mycenaean remains, ruins of a theatre and of a temple of Apollo may be seen at Damos. Medieval monuments are also abundant (castle of the Knights outside Pothia, at Chorion and elsewhere) as are churches, including that of Panaghia Chrysochera, built within the bailey of the ruined tower of the Knights. There are several monasteries, caves with spectacular stalactites and stalagmites and therapeutic springs. The loveliest region on the island is the verdant valley of Vathy.

230

Crete - *Aghios Nikolaos*

231. Crete, the largest of the Greek islands and the fourth largest in the Mediterranean, commercial and cultural crossroads since antiquity, is famed for its climate, varied landscape and its historical monuments from prehistory till recent times. Towering mountain peaks, idyllic shores, lushly verdant plains, picturesque villages, pleasant and hospitable people, create a picture of Crete which both moves and enchants. Aghios Nikolaos, located on the north coast of Crete, in a bay. With its picturesque little harbour, its houses and tree-lined streets, the town has a most attractive appearance.

Elounta

232-233. Two views of Elounta, picturesque region of Crete with its modern tourist installations built upon the ruins of ancient Olous, harbour of ancient Dreros where the famous Archaic temple of Apollo stood. At this point the peninsula of Spinalonga is joined to the coast.

232

233

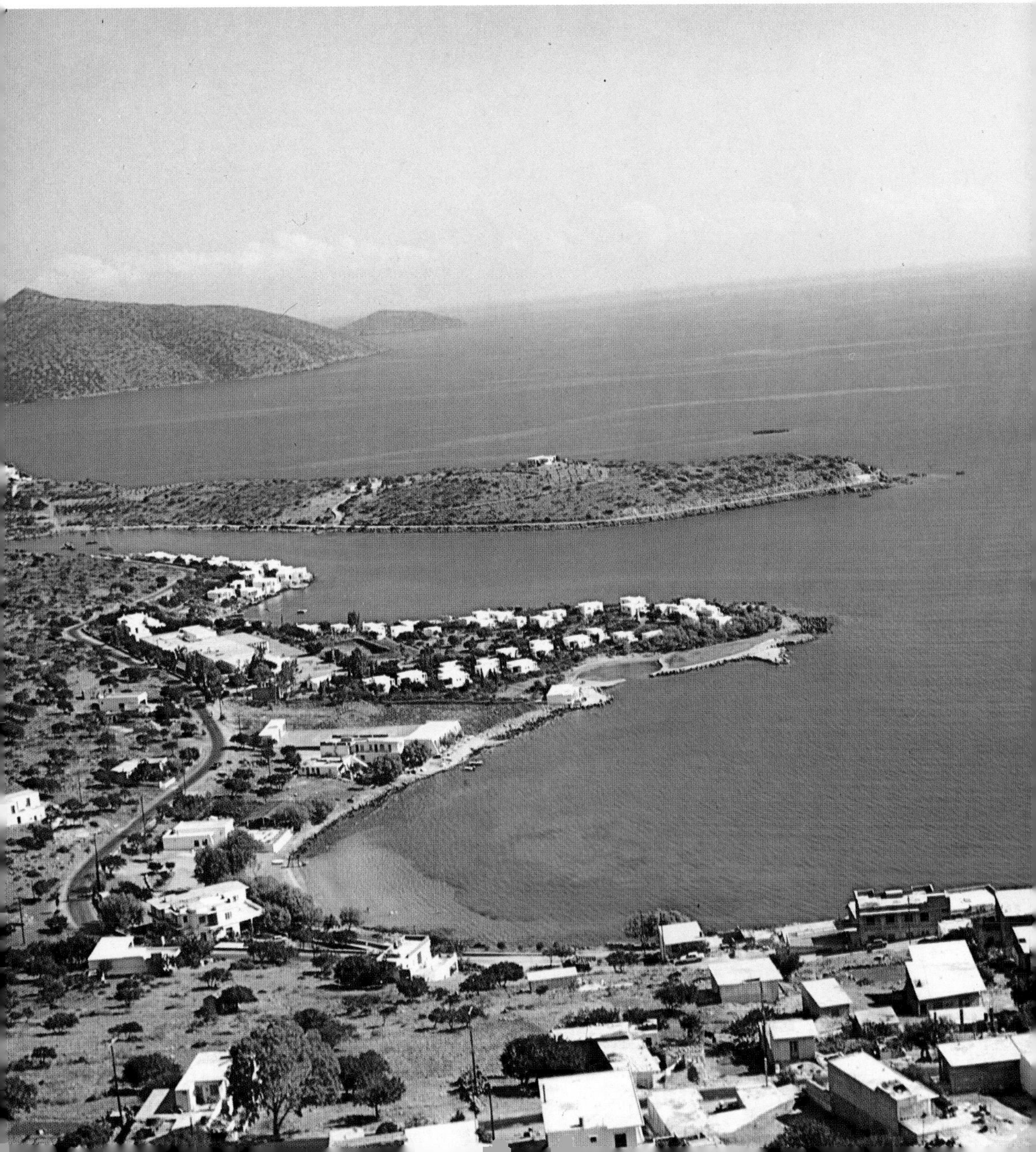

Rethymnon

234-235. Rethymnon, in western Crete, between Chania and Herakleion, is capital of the homonymous Nome (county). It is an especially interesting town, with its Venetian fortress, Fortetsa, Venetian harbour, mosques and minarets. Its environs include Anogeia, with its incomparable woven goods and idiosyncratic inhabitants. From here one ascends to the Idaean Cave, where Rhea hid the infant Zeus so that his father, Kronos, would not swallow him.

236. The Arkadi Monastery, a few kilometres outside Rethymnon. According to tradition the monastery was founded in the 11th century. It is of especial architectural interest, since its facade combines Classical, Corinthian and Baroque architectural elements. The monastery was assured of its place in history after the famous holocaust in November 1866, when it was besieged by the Turks. The Abbot Gabriel, rather than surrender, blew up part of the monastery together with the besieged. Their bones, together with vestments, are preserved to this day.

237. Frankocastello, near Sphakia, on the Libyan Sea. It was built by the Venetians in 1371 and has impressive square towers. It is linked with many local traditions.

238. Aghia Galini, a picturesque town on the Libyan Sea with a delightful harbour. It is a resort open throughout the year.

239. Paliochora, located beside the Libyan Sea, with its superb beach, high temperatures and small Venetian castle.

240. View of the very interesting town of Chora Sphakion.

241. The Samaria Gorge, a true miracle of nature, the longest and deepest in Europe. This is a region of wild magnificence and unrivalled beauty through which runs a stream which flows into the sea near Aghia Roumeli. The walls of the gorge are, in some places, quite far apart and in others only a few metres from one another. This is the home of the Cretan ibex. The little village of Samaria is located about half way along the gorge.

242. The enchanting sands of Matala. Ancient tombs carved into the rock have been found, which in Roman times were used as places of cult.

42

Chania

243-245. *Chania, capital of the homonymous Nome and of the west of Crete, is a pleasant town which preserves much of its Venetian and Turkish character. Situated on the site of ancient Kydonia, with its naturally fortified harbour, Chania is continually bustling, while its hinterland boasts one of the most haughty and proud regions of Crete, Sphakia. Home of Eleftherios Venizelos, it was in the front line in the struggle for Crete's independence and union with Greece. The old town of Chania is particularly interesting: the vaulted market place in the town centre, the ramparts and Turkish mosques, the ruined Castello, the Venetian churches of San Francesco and Aghios Rokkos, the Venetian palaces and mansions, the church of the Saviour, the museums, as well as Venizelos' house at Chalepa and his grave at Akrotiri.*

Knossos

246. Knossos. General view of the palace in which the east wing is easily visible, on the first level of which were the palace workshops and magazines. Centre of the Minoan civilisation during the second millennium BC, it consists of an enormous palatial complex, the residence of king Minos, where one is confused by the daedalic arrangement, the royal apartments with their famous wall paintings, the drainage system, the renowned labyrinth, the throne room, hall of the double axes, the queen's quarters and other building complexes. Knossos is a never ending experience.

247. *View of Knossos with the restored north wall and copy of the relief fresco of the bull.*

248. *Knossos, the south propylaia with the horns of consecration. In front of it is the South Corridor and the South Terrace.*

249. *One of the magazines with enormous pithoi lined up along the length of the walls and a row of stone "cists" beneath the floor.*

247

Herakleion

250. Herakleion, capital of the homonymous Nome and centre of Crete. The city is built in the middle of a region which includes the most important archaeological sites and most significant sights. Fortified by Spanish Saracens in 824 it was called Chandax, after a defensive moat constructed around the town. A launching base for pirates, it passed into Byzantine hands in 961 and, later, to the Venetians and Turks, the latter remaining until Crete's autonomy in 1898. There are many reminders of the past preserved in the town. Exceptionally picturesque is the old Venetian harbour, as are the walls, castle, churches, mosques and medieval monuments. Places of interest include the archaeological museum with its incomparable wealth and beauty of exhibits.

Herakleion

251. *Another view of the town of Herakleion.*

252. *The Venetian basilica of St. Mark, built in 1303, which was transformed into a mosque by the Turks. Nowadays it houses copies of ecclesiastical wall paintings and is used as a lecture and concert hall.*

253. *The Morosini Fountain, a beautiful monument of the 17th century, in the centre of a square. It was made by the Venetian ruler, Francesco Morosini and is decorated with sculpted compositions which are dated to the 14th century.*

254-255. *Herakleion. Part of the harbour and fort with vaulted arsenal.*

251

256, 258. Phaistos. Yet another extremely interesting archaeological site where a Minoan palace, similar to that at Knossos, though much smaller, has been excavated. It has the same daedalic form with a host of rooms, corridors, propylaia, staircases and ramps, which extend asymmetrically and constitute different sectors of the palace, built at different levels. Phaistos is built on an eminence overlooking the rich Mesara plain which spreads out all around. To the north is the magnificent mass of Mt. Ida and the site has a unique view over the Libyan Sea.

257. View of the archaeological site of Tylissos

256

259. One of the pithoi from the magazines at the palace of Malia.

260-261. Zakros, on the east coast of Crete. In the small village of Kato Zakro another Minoan palace has been revealed, the same as the other known palaces but smaller. Excavations have revealed wonderful finds, since the palace was unplundered.

259

Minoan civilisation

A distinctive civilisation evolved in Crete which attained its zenith between 2600 and and 1400 BC, approximately. It is distinguished both by the wealth and exceptional quality of its artistic creations, as developed in various centres throughout the island and in the palaces. Pottery, minor art objects, stone-carving, gold-work, seal-stone carving, the production of weapons, jewellery and cult objects indicate the high achievement of Minoan artists, advanced techniques, cultural level of the island, as well as its affluence and economic wealth.

262. The famous faience figurine of the Snake Goddess from Knossos. It belongs to the Neopalatial period (1700-1450 BC) and, apart from the excellent technique, furnishes us with much information about Minoan female attire.

263. Detail from the famous stone "Harvesters vase" from Aghia Triada. The detailed rendering of the movements of the figures has been achieved with exceptional vitality.

264. Rhyton in the form of a bull's head, also from Knossos. It is carved in steatite, in a markedly naturalistic manner, rendering all the strength of the sacred animal of Crete, the Bull. The inlaid eyes were of rock crystal and the horns were gilded.

265. Wall painting of bull-sports from the palace of Knossos. A whole scene from the bull-leaping contest, in which men and women participated, is illustrated.

262

210

263

264

265

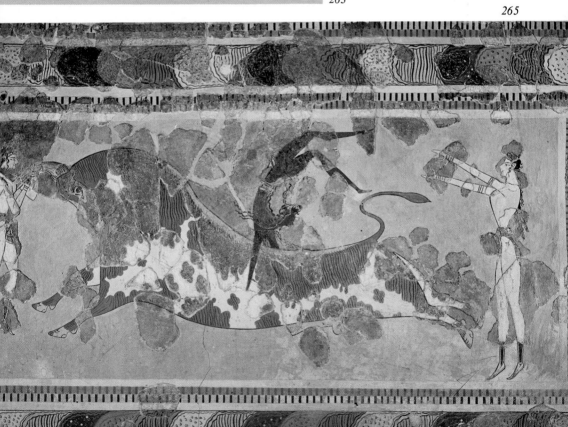